How

Taking up a
Franchise

Taking up a
Franchise

*How to buy a franchise and
make a success of it*

MATTHEW RECORD

How To Books

Published by How To Books Ltd, 3 Newtec Place,
Magdalen Road, Oxford OX4 1RE. United Kingdom.
Tel: (01865) 793806. Fax: (01865) 248780.
email: info@howtobooks.co.uk
http://www.howtobooks.co.uk

British Library Cataloguing in Publication Data.
A catalogue record for this book is available from
the British Library.

Edited by Barbara Massam
Cartoons by Mike Flanagan
Cover design by Shireen Nathoo Design
Cover image PhotoDisc

Produced for How To Books by Deer Park Productions
Typeset by PDQ Typesetting, Newcastle-under-Lyme, Staffs.
Printed and bound by Cromwell Press, Trowbridge, Wiltshire

NOTE: The material contained in this book is set out in good
faith for general guidance and no liability can be accepted
for loss or expense incurred as a result of relying in particular
circumstances on statements made in the book. Laws and
regulations are complex and liable to change, and readers should
check the current position with the relevant authorities before
making personal arrangements.

Contents

List of illustrations   8

Preface   9

1 **Defining franchising**   **11**
   Introducing franchising   11
   Understanding the types of franchise   12
   Exploring franchise potential   14
   Describing the advantages   16
   Exploring the disadvantages   18
   Case studies   19
   Action points   20

2 **Assessing yourself**   **21**
   Being honest with yourself   21
   Describing your background   22
   Utilising your skills   23
   Addressing your financial status   25
   Considering and consulting your family   26
   Case studies   29
   Action points   30

3 **Gathering information**   **31**
   Using the British Franchise Association   31
   Knowing where to look   34
   Considering your options   36
   Shortlisting the opportunities   40
   Compiling your research   41
   Case studies   42
   Action points   43

4 **Choosing the right franchise** **44**
  Attending franchise exhibitions 44
  Receiving a franchise prospectus 46
  Meeting your prospective franchisor 47
  Speaking to existing franchisees 47
  Evaluating a franchise 48
  Assessing the business proposition 50
  Case studies 51
  Action points 52

5 **Financing a franchise** **53**
  Preparing your business plan 53
  Assessing your start-up costs 56
  Raising capital 59
  Locating sources of finance 60
  Assessing your potential income 63
  Case studies 64
  Action points 65

6 **Buying a franchise** **66**
  Setting up a new franchise 66
  Taking over an existing franchise 68
  Defining your location 70
  Understanding the franchise fee 71
  Meeting the franchisor 72
  Deciding to buy 73
  The purchase agreement 75
  Case studies 76
  Action points 77

7 **Understanding the franchise agreement** **78**
  Recognising key points and clauses of the franchise
  agreement 78
  Analysing the franchise agreement 80
  Renewing your franchise agreement 82
  Case studies 82
  Action points 83

8 **Complying with legal requirements**   **84**
   Understanding the trading form of your franchise   84
   Informing the relevant authorities   86
   Keeping accounts   87
   Insuring your franchise   90
   Employing staff   91
   Case studies   94
   Action points   95

9 **Becoming a franchisee**   **96**
   Receiving your initial training   96
   Using the operating manual   97
   Surviving the first months   99
   Succeeding as a franchisee   100
   Managing your business   101
   Case studies   102
   Action points   103

10 **Running a successful franchise**   **104**
   Developing your business   104
   Maximising your business potential   105
   Recruiting the right staff   107
   Maintaining your optimum profitability   109
   Seeking professional guidance   111
   Case studies   114
   Action points   115

Glossary   116

Useful addresses   120

Further reading   123

Index   127

List of Illustrations

1. How the franchise industry is segregated in terms of business sectors 15

2. A chart showing how to assess your financial status 27

3. A checklist of key questions to ask when gathering information 38

4. A scattergram showing the elements of choosing the right franchise 44

5. A specimen letter to a potential source of finance 56

6. An organisational chart 68

7. A sample confidentiality agreement 74

8. A flow chart showing the PAYE and NI process 93

9. A chart showing a typical training programme 97

10. A sample cash-flow forecast 106

11. A sample profit and loss used to calculate break-even point 110

Preface

Franchising is often described as the world's most successful business formula. The UK franchise industry is currently worth around £7 billion, comprising over 570 alternative types of business franchise and employing some 273,000 people. A franchise is one of the safest ways to run your own business, with the success rate of a franchised business currently standing at an impressive eight out of ten. This compares with an eight out of ten failure rate for independent business start-ups.

A franchise offers tremendous scope for the individual who wishes to be self-employed, but at the same time remain part of a larger organisation. It can provide an opportunity to develop ideas and initiatives within an existing marketplace which can then be serviced through a much larger, and often national, network. Becoming part of a corporate identity can offer advantages and communications links which may be beyond the limits of an individual operating a private small business. Opportunities also exist in the franchise sector for the development of a family business.

Franchising can present the chance to develop and promote an existing business in a new area, or to improve and enhance an already well-established outlet. The spectrum is vast in every sense, with franchise businesses being available in the product-based industry as well as in the service sector. The level of investment is also wide-ranging, providing an opportunity to work with, and safeguard, your own investment in a proven field.

This book highlights the avenues to be explored before selecting and buying a franchise, followed by the methods for running and maintaining a successful franchised business. It is intended as a comprehensive guide for prospective candidates in this field.

Matthew Record

1

Defining Franchising

INTRODUCING FRANCHISING

In its broadest sense, the term *franchising* is used to describe a particular type of licensing arrangement between a business owner (a franchisor) and a business operator (a franchisee). Franchising was evident in England in the Middle Ages, in the form both of licenses granted to the peers of the country for use of land in their charge and also the early tithe system operated by the Church. This method of licensed trading was rediscovered in the United States after the Civil War, and underwent an accelerated growth period during the 1960s and 1970s. Franchising is now used throughout the world as a successful formula for companies to expand their businesses in a cost-effective way. Examples of organisations granting licences to others include:

- car manufacturers – to sell their cars
- broadcasting authorities – to run television stations
- railway companies – to operate train services
- film studios – to reproduce their merchandise
- branded clothing companies – to reproduce their logos.

Understanding the diversity of franchises

Although many licensing arrangements fall into the category of agencies or distributorships they are still referred to as franchises. It is difficult to define the term franchising in one particular meaning because it encompasses such a broad and diverse variety of businesses from a multitude of industries. Although not a partnership in the legal sense franchising can be described as such, its success being wholly dependent on both parties keeping to the franchise agreement. In recent years the term *business format franchise* has emerged to describe the universal concept of both franchising and the franchise industry.

How does it work?

In its simplest form a business format franchise operates when a franchisor agrees to sell the licensed rights of a business to a franchisee for a continuing service fee. The franchisee then operates the business in accordance with the agreed guidelines and policies of the franchisor within a specified territory. The term business format franchise is frequently referred to as a **trade mark** or **trade name franchise**.

Franchising is mutually beneficial for both franchisees and franchisors alike. In exchange for the investment of capital, time and commitment the franchisee gains a proven, low-risk independent business. The franchisor expands their network by exchanging a tried and tested business for the benefit of another outlet in a new territory with minimum capital investment.

UNDERSTANDING THE TYPES OF FRANCHISE

There are essentially six individual sectors which together comprise the business format franchise concept:

- executive franchise
- job franchise
- investment franchise
- management franchise
- retail franchise
- sales and distribution franchise.

Executive franchise

Executive franchises are traditionally geared towards the needs of business executives, such as managing directors. A franchisee operates a business providing a service in areas such as accountancy, cost reduction, project management and consultancy. Generally, the need for business premises is eliminated as the majority of the work is conducted at the client's place of work. Examples of these include Expense Reduction Analysts (ERA), David Coleman Limited and Priority Management.

Job franchise

As the name suggests, a **job franchise** operates when a franchisee purchases the right to run a one-person business. This type of franchise usually requires a lower level of financial investment than many other opportunities and is often dependent on knowledge and qualifications in a specialist field, e.g. electrician. Repair and installation, security systems and motorist services are examples of job franchises. Franchisors operating in this sector include Mac Tools, Computa Tune, Master Thatchers Ltd and Saks Hair.

Investment franchise

An investment franchise operates when a franchisee makes a substantial capital investment into a franchise concept such as a major hotel or restaurant. The franchisee retains the overall management of the enterprise with operational managers and auxiliary staff employed to carry out the day-to-day running of the business. Companies such as Greenalls Inn Partnership, Wimpy and Holiday Inns are examples of these.

Management franchise

This type of franchise involves a franchisee managing and co-ordinating a group of operatives throughout several territories or within a defined region. Van-based service franchises such as ServiceMaster, Molly Maids and Chemical Express are examples of these.

Retail franchise

With a retail franchise, a franchisee would be expected to make a large financial investment in business premises, fittings, equipment and employees in order to operate a high-turnover business system. Unlike an investment franchise, retail franchises are generally operated on an owner-operator basis. High street shops such as Kall Kwik, McDonald's and Swinton Insurance are examples of retail franchises.

Sales and distribution franchise

A sales and distribution franchise operates with the franchisee on the road selling and distributing products direct to clients. As the customer base or territory increases, additional vehicles and staff can be employed to cope with the growth. Amtrak Express Parcels, Video Select and Dairy Crest are examples of these.

The type of franchise most suited to your personal needs and objectives will be influenced by your financial level of investment combined with your level of interest. Whether you prefer a hands-on approach or are seeking an investment opportunity, the diversity of the franchise industry will ensure that there is an opportunity available that meets your individual criteria.

EXPLORING FRANCHISE POTENTIAL

Franchising is often described as the world's most successful business formula. A recent survey, jointly conducted by the National Westminster Bank and the British Franchise Association (the BFA), revealed that the continued growth of franchising has had a positive effect on the British economy. The British business format franchise sector generates an annual turnover estimated at £7 billion and employs over 273,000 people. There are currently more than 570 business format franchisors offering a multitude of investment opportunities ranging from a few thousand pounds to hundreds of thousands of pounds.

Combining a proven business formula with independent self-employment has established franchising as a relatively low-risk way into business. A franchise is one of the safest ways to run your own business with the success rate in this field currently standing at an impressive eight out of ten. This compares with an eight out of ten failure rate for independent business start-ups. Ninety-two per cent of franchised businesses generate a profit and attribute their success to:

- ensuring consistent customer satisfaction
- selling a good product or providing a good service
- working hard.

Comparing sectors of the franchise industry

In recent years, hotels and catering, personal services and store retailing have emerged as the largest sectors within the franchising industry. Figure 1 shows how the franchise industry is segregated in terms of business sector and is reproduced from the findings of the Nat West/BFA survey, courtesy of the BFA.

Suitability of a franchisee

The franchise industry does not discriminate against age or gender but considers self-motivation, financial acumen, determination and a positive attitude towards work essential in achieving long-term success. The level of profitability of a chosen franchise will almost certainly be a reflection of the effort contributed to the business.

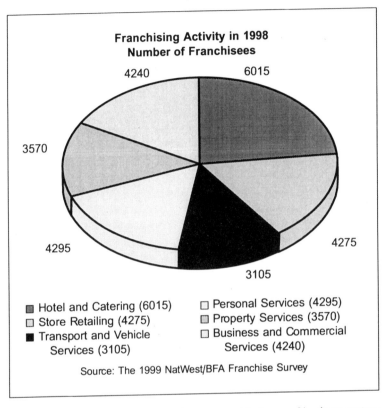

**Franchising Activity in 1998
Number of Franchisees**

- ▨ Hotel and Catering (6015)
- ☐ Store Retailing (4275)
- ■ Transport and Vehicle
  Services (3105)
- ☐ Personal Services (4295)
- ▨ Property Services (3570)
- ☐ Business and Commercial
  Services (4240)

Source: The 1999 NatWest/BFA Franchise Survey

Fig. 1. How the franchise industry is segregated in terms of business sectors (Courtesy of the British Franchise Association).

Franchisees can be categorised into three different types:

1. Top performers – these fully exploit the franchise potential and excel in their chosen business by exceeding all forecasts and projections.

2. Average performers – these will do just enough to achieve their objectives and generate sufficient profit to maintain their business.

3. Below average performers – these believe it is the responsibility of the franchisor to generate sales and build up the business, making no effort to expand their business within their own area.

Applying commitment

If you are considering taking up a franchise then obviously your aim will be to become a top performer. In order to achieve this you must be certain that you can not only apply a high level of commitment to your venture but are capable of sustaining it. This requires a brutally honest assessment of yourself and your circumstances. We look at this in more detail in Chapter 2. Making sure that the franchise you have chosen is the right one for you is of paramount importance both in terms of your ability and application and your interest in that type of business. It is difficult to achieve a top performance level in any career unless you enjoy what you are doing and gain job satisfaction from it. Goals and targets can be reached more easily with a genuine keenness and wish to succeed. It is this determination which will also enable you to cope with the problems and obstacles that are bound to occur if you are running any business. Chapter 4 looks in more detail at selecting the most suitable franchise for you.

To avoid falling into the category of the below average performers you must not expect to take up a franchise thinking that you have a ready-made business that will run itself. The resources and advice provided by the franchisor will not present you with a profitable business that just needs managing but will give you the basis on which to build and develop. Being successfully self-employed makes no allowance for complacency.

DESCRIBING THE ADVANTAGES

Receiving specialist training

The advantages associated with the concept of franchising are simply not evident with independent business start-ups. For example, the franchisor's initial and continued specialised training programme enables new and inexperienced franchisees to become competent operators within their chosen business in a comparatively short space of time. This specialised knowledge benefits the franchisor and franchisee alike.

Using an established brand name

The ongoing help and guidance of the franchisor has helped make franchising the world renowned success it has become. Many franchisors have established themselves as brand names, including market leaders such as McDonald's and Prontaprint. A franchise with such a company immediately provides you with a nationally held reputation on which to build your business.

Raising capital
A franchised business will usually require less start-up capital than an independent business as the franchisor has usually already investigated the market through pilot operations. In addition, the franchisor will be able to offer advice on issues such as the suitability of trading location, optimum stock levels, staff training, equipment purchase and accountancy.

Being part of a larger organisation
A popular saying describes the franchising concept as *'an opportunity to be in business for yourself but not by yourself'*. Becoming part of a larger organisation as opposed to working alone can be advantageous in itself. For example, advertising can be a major but necessary expense to any business, particularly a new one. However, in exchange for a contribution towards marketing, franchisees benefit from cost-effective advertising throughout the marketplace of the entire network. This philosophy of pooling resources for everyone's benefit can apply to other areas of the business such as bulk purchasing and the shared use of market information collated by the franchisor.

Introducing new products or services
The costs associated with research and development leading to the introduction of new products or services are undertaken by the franchisor. This in turn allows franchisees the use of trade marks, copyrights, patents and trade secrets. These factors all increase the credibility and reputation of the franchisee in developing their own business.

Reducing business risk
A major advantage with franchising is the reduction of business risk, although the market is not guaranteed and no business is ever completely risk-free. However, franchising relies on proven business systems and the recognised success of franchising has helped lenders look favourably towards financing a franchise opportunity.

EXPLORING THE DISADVANTAGES

As with any business, franchising has its disadvantages.

The constraints of the franchise agreement

As a franchisee you will be required to operate your business in accordance with the constraints of the franchise agreement. The controls imposed by the franchisor will affect every aspect of your business, from purchase and operation through to sale or transfer. For any franchise system to work successfully it is the responsibility of all franchisees to adhere to the rules and regulations stipulated by the franchisor. Although these controls are imposed to regulate the quality of service or products, they can often restrict your own objectives when taking up a franchise. Franchising is a team effort, and before embarking on this type of business venture you should weigh carefully your ability to operate as an efficient and effective member of a team.

Continuing costs

A franchised business incurs continued costs beyond the initial franchise fee. The initial fee enables the franchisee to make use of the franchisor's services and to operate the business system. However, a franchisor will demand a continuing fee usually in the form of a percentage of turnover. This is where a conflict often occurs. A franchisor may increase selling prices as a means of increasing turnover, thereby generating larger fees from franchisees. In contrast, this may not be beneficial to the franchisee, who may feel that the customer base cannot withstand price increases and who would prefer to achieve increased profitability by improved efficiency and decreased overheads. A franchisor may decide to update and modernise equipment used in the overall running of the network, thereby forcing franchisees to do the same to remain compatible. This may result in major expenditure and is another source of potential conflict.

Selling your franchise

The controls governing how a business should be run also apply to how and to whom you are able to sell or transfer your business. When a franchisor initially sells a franchise, a great deal of time and effort is spent ensuring the franchisee is suitable to operate the business. So when you sell or transfer your business the franchisor will undertake a similar assessment to ensure your replacement meets the same criteria. The sale of a franchise will incur fees payable to the franchisor, to cover the cost of dealing with applicants and training new franchisees. Additionally, an introduction fee may be imposed by the franchisor if the new franchisee originated as a direct result of their actions.

Assessing the qualities of the franchisor

Not all franchised businesses are well-established and therefore it may be difficult to assess fully the quality of your potential franchisor (Chapter 4, Choosing the Right Franchise, deals with this in more detail). Even though franchisors are encouraged to market-test new products and services through their company-owned outlets, they are not infallible and errors of judgement can occur. The cost of a failed new product or service could be partially borne by franchisees and may affect the reputation of the business.

Becoming dependent upon your franchisor

As a franchisee it can be easy to fall into a false sense of security and in turn become dependent on the franchisor. This reliance on the franchisors together with the imposition of controls and regulations, may negate the feeling of independence so that the franchisee loses enthusiasm and incentive. This is detrimental to the long-term success of the business and is opposed to the principle of franchising.

CASE STUDIES

Joshua decides to sell his franchise

Joshua is 40 years old, married with two children and has successfully run his contract cleaning business, 'Clean and Gleam', for the past five years. He originally bought the home-based franchise for £10,000 and achieved a £25,000 turnover with 15 per cent net profit during his first year of trading. Annual turnover has increased to £250,000 and his net profit is now at 25 per cent. He has leased a large industrial unit, employs 15 staff and runs a fleet of ten vehicles. Joshua's success has been the direct result of hard work, long hours and careful business planning. However, Joshua considers he has taken the business as far as he can, and the time has come to sell his business and move on.

Jake considers franchising

Jake is 30 years old, single and lives in his own house. Jake has worked within the electrical industry since leaving school. He completed his apprenticeship with a small local electrical company before becoming self-employed four years ago following unexpected redundancy. Since becoming self-employed he has enjoyed moderate success but has always felt he could achieve more with a large brand name behind him. Jake feels that an electrical-based franchise will utilise his existing skills and experience whilst allowing him to be in business for himself but not by himself.

Charlotte wants to buy a business

Charlotte is 25 years old and has her own home. She has always been highly self-motivated and has been working ever since her first part-time job delivering newspapers when she was just eleven. At present she is the assistant manager of a video rental shop and combined with money left to her in a will has managed to accumulate nearly £15,000 in savings. She has realised that she has the drive and ambition to become her own boss and is looking to acquire a franchise opportunity geared around her favourite pastime, the world of entertainment.

ACTION POINTS

1. Make sure that you fully understand the franchising concept and ensure that it is ideal for you.

2. Be willing to work as part of a team and accept the working regulations and restrictions within your own business.

3. Know which type of franchise will be most suitable for your proposed level of investment and commitment.

2

Assessing Yourself

BEING HONEST WITH YOURSELF

As with any business a franchise will demand a substantial amount of your time, energy and in many cases financial investment. It is for these very reasons that you must be fully committed to running your own business and under no misconception of exactly what is involved. The first stage of this process is to be honest with yourself. If you are not then the only person you deceive will be yourself.

Your personal health and fitness

As strong as it may be, to simply have a desire to be your own boss, or a willingness to work hard, will not be enough to run your own business. Very few people entering self-employment for the first time are fully aware of exactly what qualities are necessary to succeed. For example, the long hours you may have worked occasionally as an employee will very quickly become a regular routine. Time off for holidays or sickness will be virtually impossible, particularly in the early stages of the business. So your personal health and fitness should be of paramount importance when considering self-employment.

Dealing with administration

It is not only the work itself that will make demands on your time, but the additional and often overlooked tasks such as answering correspondence, dealing with administration, chasing up suppliers, invoicing clients, keeping accounts and organising the general day-to-day running of the business. If your business is a one-person operation then these tasks will be your responsibility alone. If you intend, and are able, to employ staff then although your workload may be reduced it will be your responsibility to manage your employees and ensure that optimum efficiency is achieved and maintained.

Taking authority

Employing and organising staff is an area in which many people starting out in business have little or no previous experience. As a franchisee you will be expected to lead by example and conduct yourself in a manner which will ensure that the standards of your business are upheld by your employees. As an employer you will have to make decisions that may not always be popular and it is essential that you manage your staff in such a way that any decisions you make will be respected by them. You should consider your ability to convey an authoritative approach. This does not mean ruling your staff with an iron rod but does include being able to discipline them and, if necessary, carry out dismissal.

Understanding how your potential franchise works

One of the most important aspects of being honest with yourself is evaluating your personal suitability for the type of work you are contemplating. For example, if you don't enjoy driving or dealing with people then a mobile distribution franchise is not for you. If you are not totally committed to the service you provide or the products you sell then this will be reflected in your work. It is essential that you understand the full workings of the business you are considering. Your decision must be made only after having fully investigated what is involved and how the business works and must not be based on a misplaced view of what you think it will be like.

This section has not been written to put you off becoming self-employed but to help you understand what you are undertaking. The following chapters will take you through the necessary steps and investigations which will help you make the right decision for you.

DESCRIBING YOUR BACKGROUND

Your particular background will influence the type of business for which you will be most suited. As a franchisee, you will be the master of your own destiny and, as such, your success or failure will be determined by your suitability. Regardless of how attractive a particular opportunity appears to be, if you have any reservations about whether or not you will enjoy the work, then do not even contemplate proceeding any further. Being brutally honest with yourself at the outset will help to avoid any potentially expensive mistakes.

Seeing franchising as a partnership

Running a franchise is a two-way **partnership** and both the franchisor and you must be equally convinced of your ability to operate the business successfully in accordance with the operating manual. Although your previous work-related background may demonstrate your potential, this only forms part of the selection process. A franchisor will consider general business experience, particularly in selling or marketing, to be advantageous, but your personal characteristics will be as important. The criteria for an ideal franchisee should include:

- being highly self-motivated and able to reach decisions on your own

- having a positive attitude towards work and all work-related tasks

- possessing a strong determination to succeed in every aspect of the business

- being able to demonstrate a high level of financial acumen.

Facing realities

Although your previous background may include a managerial position, franchising is very much a hands-on type of business and, as such, the type of tasks you used to delegate will probably now be undertaken by you. Your background will only form a base to build on and you will be constantly learning and developing new skills. Any preconception of buying a business and letting others do the work whilst you sit back and take all the profits must be eliminated at the outset.

UTILISING YOUR SKILLS

Your reasons for contemplating a particular type of franchise may be influenced by the skills you already have. Utilising existing skills can be beneficial to both you and your franchisor. Knowledge of the business you are considering will be a valuable insight providing the self-confidence you will need to tackle your new venture.

Although most franchises are designed to be run with little or no previous experience, there are exceptions to this rule. For example, businesses which require a certain level of technical expertise, such as car mechanics or electrical work, are very often initially a one-man operation and without the necessary qualifications in that specialist field, cannot be successfully operated.

It is still important, however, to remember that running any business means undertaking tasks on a multitude of levels and the physical ability to do a job only forms one part of the equation. In addition to your direct work-related skills you will need to be able to do the following:

- work with and motivate people
- communicate with people
- adapt to the responsibility of new tasks such as invoicing, tax and PAYE.

Assessing the value of your previous skills

First-hand experience within a particular business sector is not always an advantage. How beneficial your previous skills and experience prove will depend on the attitude of you and your franchisor towards one another. For example, if you have worked in a particular industry for a number of years your franchisor may consider that you are set in your ways. You may not be receptive to the working practices of the business, believing that you cannot be taught anything new. Alternatively another franchisor may consider your experience to be a valuable asset to the business. This will be reinforced if you can show that you are adaptable and responsive to new methods and improvements. The exchange of knowledge and ideas has to be a two-way arrangement whereby both parties benefit for the good of the business.

Evaluating your skills for the business you want

When considering your proposed franchise you need to evaluate your skills in terms of what is needed to run the business. It is rare that someone embarking on a new enterprise is able to rely totally on existing skills. Regardless of how comprehensive your background may be there will be limitations in your ability to run your chosen business. So it is important that you have the incentive to develop and apply your current knowledge. This will ensure that you can cover all aspects of the business.

Applying your skills

Utilising your skills does not mean only applying your strengths but also having the ability to recognise your weaknesses. Whilst it is possible to acquire new skills proficiently you must ensure that you have sufficient time and resources to do this. In areas totally unfamiliar to you it may be more beneficial, and more cost effective, to employ someone, leaving yourself free for other tasks.

ADDRESSING YOUR FINANCIAL STATUS

Your financial status will naturally affect the type of business you are able to purchase. There may be quite a difference between the type of business you would like to buy and the type you can afford to buy. Your dream to purchase a major fast food franchise may be a little ambitious if you do not have the financial resources to back it up. Even though banks generally perceive the franchise industry in a positive light, it is important not to stretch yourself financially. Chapter 5, Financing a Franchise, examines this in greater detail. Although it sounds obvious, you should never borrow more money than you can comfortably afford to repay.

Exercising caution
It is all too easy to believe that a particular business is the best opportunity ever likely to come along and must be purchased at all costs. However, no matter how attractive the proposition appears to be caution must be exercised when undertaking any financial commitment. If possible try to take a step back from the situation and ask yourself if it really is as good as it appears. Do not let yourself get so involved with an opportunity that overenthusiasm for the venture prevents you from making sound judgements based on logic and common sense. Before committing yourself to anything talk to as many unbiased people as you can and only when you are 100 per cent sure in your own mind should you continue. Avoid talking to friends at all costs. Even the best of intentions have a habit of turning sour and, at the end of the day, it is your money and you will have to live with the consequences, good or bad.

Raising additional funds
Some franchises require a substantial capital investment and unless you are fortunate enough to have sufficient personal savings you will need to raise additional funds. Banks will generally lend up to 70 per cent towards the purchase price of a franchise. However, depending on the level of investment and your personal circumstances the bank may ask for your home as security for the loan. Therefore, it is imperative that your family are fully committed to

the business and understand the implications.

Beware of attempting to impress a potential franchisor or lender by claiming to have more money than you actually have. This will do little to enhance your working relationship when the truth is revealed and may be disastrous if you need help with raising finance at some time in the future. It is always better to be honest at the beginning than look a fool at a later date. Figure 2 uses the example of Joshua's financial status to give guidance on assessing your own.

A simple financial checklist

1. **How much will the business cost?**
    No matter how carefully you calculate the cost of buying a business there will always be unforeseen expenses and you should always try to make provision for these hidden costs.

2. **How much money do you personally have?**
    Any family loans should be excluded at this stage.

3. **How will the rest of the money be financed and under what terms?**
    If you intend to borrow money from family or friends then it is still advisable to get the terms of the loan in writing to avoid an unexpected demand for instant repayment which you cannot meet.

CONSIDERING AND CONSULTING YOUR FAMILY

If you have a family then buying a business is a decision which you cannot make in isolation. Self-employment will affect every aspect of family life, from the initial financial investment through to the day-to-day running of the business. So, before reaching any conclusive decision it is imperative that you consider and consult your immediate family. Running a business is a difficult undertaking in itself and does not need the additional complications of family disputes. It is important that your family is aware of the commitment you are making to your new business and that they are happy and willing to make the same commitment to you. Without this support and understanding it will be difficult to succeed.

Considering the financial strains

The prime family issue will probably be finance. As previously

ASSESSMENT OF JOSHUA'S FINANCIAL STATUS

ASSETS:	£
Property	
Independent value of house	120,000
Independent value of other property (business lease)	5,000
Business	
Estimated value of business	95,000
Insurance and savings	
Value of insurance policies (if surrendered)	2,500
Cash savings	10,000
ISAs	3,000
Bonds	
Stocks	
Shares	8,000
Unit Trusts	
Investments	
Additional assets	
Estimated value of vehicles	11,000
Other assets that can be sold (paintings, antiques)	2,500
Total Assets	**257,000**

LIABILITIES	
Outstanding mortgages	
Private home	95,000
Business premises	
Balance of existing loans	
Personal loan	850
Hire Purchase	2,000
Leases	
Outstanding credit/debit card balance	
Credit cards	350
Debit cards	
Store cards	250
Other financial commitments	
Business overdraft	5,200
Regular payments	1,200
Total Liabilities	**104,850**
NET WORTH	
Total assets less total liabilities	**152,150**

Fig. 2. A chart showing how to assess your financial status.

mentioned, a substantial financial investment may be required and if you intend to invest a proportion of your joint savings or perhaps use your home as security, the full support and agreement of your spouse or partner is essential. Any change in your financial situation may bring additional pressures into the family environment which have not previously been encountered. If you are making the transition from employed to self-employed your family will no longer have the security of a regular wage but you will still have to meet your existing financial commitments. These will be essential items such as mortgage repayments, direct debits and general housekeeping expenses, including food and clothes. In addition to all of this there will be new expenses generated by the business.

Understanding the strain on relationships

Until the business becomes established, work-related tasks will often take precedence over family affairs and this can put a strain on relationships. The things you used to take for granted such as paid holidays may have to be postponed indefinitely or at least until you feel confident to entrust your business to someone else. During this time you and your family have to accept that guaranteed free time is not possible, not only in respect of annual holidays, but work may also intrude on weekends, bank holidays etc.

If possible, try to get the family involved in certain aspects of the business. Not only will this alleviate some of the pressure but it may prove invaluable if you become ill or unable to work. Simple, time-consuming tasks such as sealing envelopes or filing paperwork can be undertaken by younger members of the family who are always eager to help. More involved tasks such as invoicing could perhaps be shared with a partner or spouse. Involving family members in this way will help them feel as though they are a part of the business and they will also understand the necessity of maintaining the agreed commitment if the business is to succeed.

Coping with family pressures

As with any new business, the initial trading weeks will be the most difficult you are ever likely to face. This is the time when the support and understanding of your family will be more important than ever. Work must take priority and when a problem arises which needs your immediate attention it may mean that a family outing has to be cancelled. There will be occasions when this is inevitable and everybody will be under pressure to resolve the situation. At these times your family support will be put to the test. It is easy to say that you are prepared for this eventuality but you have to be certain that you can cope with it when it happens. Both your commitment, and your family's commitment must be total and will be worthless if, when the possibility becomes a reality, you cannot honour it.

CASE STUDIES

Joshua considers his options

Joshua's business has been independently valued at £95,000. He needs to consider his options carefully before he totally commits to selling. He could choose between selling the business outright or selling just a percentage. If he sells outright then he can either buy another business or invest his money. By selling a percentage he would be able to spend more time with his family and still retain an interest in the business he has worked hard to build up. With so many decisions to make Joshua decides to take some time away from the business. This will enable to him to fully assess his position and decide on the best course of action.

Jake investigates the franchise market

Jake is new to franchising and needs to find out as much information as he possibly can about the industry. He begins his search at the local library where he finds a wide variety of franchise books and magazines. All of the information he reads advises him how invaluable franchise exhibitions are as a source of up-to-date information. From the information he reads Jake is able to determine which type of business would be best suited to his needs. Before contacting potential franchisors individually he decides to attend a forthcoming exhibition to learn more about the opportunities on offer.

Charlotte examines her options

Although Charlotte does not have a particular trade or skill she is able to draw on her managerial experience which she feels will be beneficial in running her own business. Charlotte is fortunate to have access to the internet and has been able to examine her franchising options online. Just like books or magazines, the internet offers a vast array of information. Charlotte finds the website of the British Franchise Association particularly helpful, with information covering all aspects of the industry. As with most sites on the internet the BFA website has links to other useful sites and Charlotte discovers that a national franchise exhibition is due to take place shortly.

ACTION POINTS

1. Be totally honest with yourself about your suitability for your chosen business.

2. Ensure that you have the necessary skills, attitude and application.

3. Make sure that you, and your family, are fully committed to your business proposal.

3

Gathering Information

USING THE BRITISH FRANCHISE ASSOCIATION (BFA)

The **British Franchise Association** (BFA) has been established as a self-regulating body for business format franchises throughout the United Kingdom. It is not compulsory for franchisors to become members of the BFA and in fact there are many reputable franchisors who are not. However, members have to conform to stringent policies and procedures devised by the BFA to set universal standards throughout the franchise industry. Membership is a prestigious accolade which is only available to companies able to meet the BFA's criteria. The BFA produces an official information pack which is available to all prospective franchisees for a fee. The pack is written as an introduction to franchising and gives prospective franchisees an insight into the industry.

Applying to the BFA

There are three principal categories under which companies can apply to become a member of the BFA:

1. **Provisional** – for companies in the process of developing the structure of their opportunity in association with accredited professional advice.

2. **Associate** – for companies who have financed and managed a successful pilot scheme for at least 12 months. In addition, they must be able to provide evidence of successful franchising over a one-year period with at least one franchisee.

3. **Full** – for companies who have financed and managed a successful pilot scheme for at least 12 months. In addition, they must provide evidence of successful franchising over a two-year period with a minimum of four franchisees.

Understanding the criteria

The criteria governing admission to the BFA stipulates that provisional and associate members must be able to demonstrate that:

- the business is viable and able to support a franchised network whilst operating at a profit
- the operating units of the business are capable of being successfully replicated
- the terms of the contract between the prospective franchisee and the franchisor comply with the European Code of Ethics
- the recruitment literature relating to the franchise opportunity represents an accurate and realistic account of the franchise proposition.

In addition to these requirements, full members must be able to demonstrate that:

- they have a proven trading and franchising record covering a minimum two-year period.

Of the three categories only full members are entitled to use the Association's logo.

Knowing the benefits of the BFA

Membership of the BFA clearly identifies companies who not only offer ethical business format franchises but also agree to undertake an ongoing commitment to uphold the Association's high standards of conduct. In addition to the advice and guidance available through accredited professional advisers, the BFA represents the commercial interests of the franchise community by helping to ensure its members are protected from unwarranted legislation in both the UK and Europe. Belonging to a BFA-endorsed franchised network is an excellent selling point for a franchisee when the time comes to resell the business.

The BFA organises various exhibitions and seminars to promote the business opportunities of its members and all exhibitors and speakers at such events conform to their standards. (Chapter 4, Choosing The Right Franchise, deals with franchise exhibitions in greater detail.) In association with HSBC (formerly known as the

Midland Bank) and the *Daily Express*, the BFA organises the Franchisee of the Year Awards. A franchisor nominates a franchisee who must then submit a 1000-word written entry indicating why they deserve to win, based on the criteria set out in the official entry form.

The National Franchisee Forum

The **National Franchisee Forum** was launched at the National Franchise Exhibition in October 1997. Its objective is to involve the franchisees of members in the BFA's work in the regulation and promotion of ethical franchising throughout the United Kingdom. The Forum is a self-funding organisation and all generated revenue is dedicated to pursuing the objectives of the Forum. The benefits for franchisees who join the Forum include:

- being consulted on topics of general interest in franchising

- enhancing the reputation of franchising by promoting the benefits for consumers of buying from franchisees

- receiving a Certificate of Participation

- being involved in the BFA's plans to gain national professional recognition for franchising as a separate and distinguished management skill

- use of the Franchise Re-Sales Register, accessed via the Franchise Forum website, designed for participants wanting to realise the capital value of their franchise

- discounted *Daily Telegraph* advertising

- group purchasing schemes

- access to a free 24-hour tax helpline.

The National Franchise Forum can be contacted through the BFA at the address below.

Contacting the BFA

The British Franchise Association can be contacted at Thames View, Newtown Road, Henley-on-Thames, Oxon RG9 1HG, telephone: (01491) 578050. If you have access to the internet then the BFA can be reached at:

- E-mail – mailroom@british-franchise.org.uk.
- Website – http://www.british-franchise.org.uk.

The website is sponsored by the five leading banks, National Westminster, Lloyds TSB, The Royal Bank of Scotland, HSBC and Barclays and is a wealth of information for anyone considering franchising.

KNOWING WHERE TO LOOK

With such a vast array of franchise opportunities currently available, finding the perfect business can prove extremely difficult. Second only to buying a home, choosing your own franchised business is likely to be the largest financial investment of your life and any mistakes made at the outset are likely to be very expensive to rectify. So that you can make a carefully calculated decision you need to learn as much about franchising as you possibly can. The following list will help you begin your quest for information:

- magazines
- advisory publications
- franchise exhibitions
- books
- library
- the internet
- interactive CD-ROM.

Reading magazines

There are a number of magazines devoted purely to the franchise industry including *Business Franchise Magazine*, the official BFA journal, and those listed below. These magazines advertise current franchise opportunities and also report on the franchise industry as a whole, regularly interviewing franchisees about their experiences:

Business Franchise Magazine, Blenheim House, 630 Chiswick High Road, London W4 5BG. Tel: (01925) 724326

The Franchise Magazine, Castle House, Castle Meadows, Norwich NR2 1PJ. Tel: (01603) 620301.

Franchise World, James House, 37 Nottingham Road, London SW17 7EA. Tel: (0208) 767 1371.

The *United Kingdom Franchise Directory* published by *The Franchise Magazine* is also an excellent source of advice and information. The directory will enable you to compare individual franchisors and includes many advisory features covering areas such as:

- the cost of buying a franchise
- buying, leasing and renting commercial property
- raising finance
- franchising and the law
- ongoing fees.

Obtaining advisory literature

In addition to the publications mentioned in the last section, and that supplied by the BFA (already discussed), a wealth of **advisory literature** (often free of charge), is available from a number of sources including:

- franchise consultants
- banks
- government agencies
- lawyers
- accountants
- exhibitions.

In conjunction with National Westminster Bank the British Franchise Association compiles an annual survey to present an accurate statistical picture of the franchise industry in the United Kingdom. The findings of this survey are available by contacting: Nat West/BFA Franchise Survey at the BFA.

If your prospective franchisor is not a member of the BFA then you should research the opportunity beyond the information provided in their recruitment literature. An excellent and cost-effective research method is to contact the cuttings libraries of newspapers in your franchisor's locality and request any relevant articles involving your franchisor. They will either forward their findings or invite you to browse through their library.

Using the internet

The following internet sites will provide you with a wealth of useful information:

Bang & Olufsen	www.b&o.com
Bond-A-Frame	www.townchoice.co.uk/bondaframe
Bounders Brucherie	www.lds.co.uk/franchise/bounders/
Burger King	www.burgerking.com
Cash Generator	www.cash.generator@thruthe.net
Chips Away	www.chipsaway.co.uk
Domino's Pizza	www.dominos.co.uk
Drinkmaster	www.drinkmaster.com
Elite Introductions	www.eliteintroductions.com
FastSigns	www.fastsigns.com
Fatty Arbuckles	www.fatty-arbuckles.co.uk
Greenalls Inn Partnerships	www.greenalls.franchise.co.uk
Humana International	www.humana-int.com
Kall Kwik Printing	www.kallkwik.co.uk
Lady of America	www.ladyofamerica.com
McDonald's Restaurants	www.mcdonalds.com
Molly Maid	www.mollymaid.com
O'Brien's	www.obriens.ie
Pirtek	www.pirtek.usa.com
Snap-On Tools	www.snap-on.com
ServiceMaster	www.servicemaster.com
Thrifty Car Rental	www.thrifty.com
Urban Planters	www.urban.yorks.com
Ventrolla	www.ventrolla.co.uk

Interactive CD-ROM

In addition to the information available from the internet a company called CDFEX has produced the world's first interactive franchise exhibition and directory on CD-ROM, exclusively endorsed by the BFA. Not only does the program enable you to compare franchise opportunities by investment levels and industry sector but you can also produce your own list of potential opportunities. Further information can be obtained from CDFEX at 78 Carlton Place, Glasgow G5 9TH. Tel: (0141) 429 5900. E-mail: sales@cdfex.com. Website: www.cdfex.com.

CONSIDERING YOUR OPTIONS

By now you should be starting to accumulate a lot of information or at least know where to begin your search. But with so much information, just how do you compare the opportunities on offer and determine which should be investigated further? It is unlikely that you will be able to learn all you need to know simply by reading about a business. Preparing the right questions to be directed to the right people will help eliminate unsuitable opportunities and highlight any possibilities.

As you begin considering your options, ask yourself whether you would buy the products or use the service on offer. If not, then why not? Are the prices too high, is the quality inferior or is there insufficient demand in your area? Although not everyone will share your viewpoint, you can use your answers as a guide to whether or not other people would spend their money with you.

At this stage one of your main objectives is to discover the effect of the operational methods employed by the franchisor on the business. This will help you to ascertain whether a particular opportunity is actually worth pursuing. To be effective, your questions need to be direct and to the point.

Asking the right questions
Your questions should cover the following topics:

- the trading history of the franchisor relating to both successes and failures

- details of how the franchisor organises and operates their business

- how much the business will cost and a breakdown detailing exactly what you get for your money

- what methods are used to calculate the financial projections and how accurate they are

- whether the franchisor can arrange finance and under what terms

- any obligations governing the purchase of corporate items

- how the franchisor makes his money

- what initial and ongoing training and services are provided, where and at what cost

- what marketing and advertising methods are used and what your contribution would be

- your obligations to your franchisor and your franchisor's obligations to you

BEFORE YOU BUY A FRANCHISE...
THE PROSPECTIVE FRANCHISEE CHECKLIST

FRANCHISEE PROSPECTUS SHOULD CONTAIN...

- [ ] Identifying data on the franchisor
- [ ] Directors' and key executives' business experience
- [ ] Company's track record
- [ ] Description of the franchise
- [ ] Initial investment required
- [ ] Other payments due to the franchisor
- [ ] Data on help in raising finance
- [ ] Restrictions on franchisee's conduct of business
- [ ] Level of franchisee's personal participation
- [ ] Termination/renewal of agreement terms
- [ ] Number of existing franchisees and their success rates
- [ ] Franchisor's rights to select/approve sites
- [ ] Training and support guaranteed to the franchisee
- [ ] Financial information about pilot operation
- [ ] Financial data on the franchisor
- [ ] List of franchisor's banker and other professional advisers

WHAT TO FIND OUT FROM FRANCHISOR...

- [ ] Company's financial health and history
- [ ] How long it has been franchising
- [ ] Details of pilot operation results
- [ ] Current number of franchisees
- [ ] Permission to talk to random franchisees
- [ ] Main source of company earnings
- [ ] Value and appeal of product or service
- [ ] Long term viability of product/service
- [ ] Type and level of head office support
- [ ] Full details of the training provided
- [ ] Whether training is an extra cost
- [ ] Total cost of taking up the franchise
- [ ] Realistic working capital needed
- [ ] Permission for bank references and other referees
- [ ] Territorial practices and exclusivity terms
- [ ] Types and amounts of advertising support
- [ ] Any need to buy products from the franchisor
- [ ] Target obligations
- [ ] Realistic P&L figures
- [ ] Management service fees or royalty payments
- [ ] Operating restrictions
- [ ] Launch assistance
- [ ] Sample contract

FRANCHISE CONTRACT MUST COVER...

- ☐ Your rights to sell or transfer ownership of the franchise
- ☐ Geographical areas and types of customers to whom you may sell
- ☐ Nature and extent of your obligations to the franchisor, including buying supplies and services
- ☐ Rights to renew or extend contract beyond the original term
- ☐ Terms and conditions under which you may terminate the contract
- ☐ Description of exact training and support the franchisor must provide
- ☐ Precise definition of price, commissions, rental fees, leases needed to own and operate the franchise
- ☐ Precise boundaries of the territory awarded to you
- ☐ Description of your heir's rights in the event of your death

BE WARY IF THE FRANCHISOR...

- ☐ Promises huge profits with thin investments
- ☐ Says 'act now to get in on the ground floor'
- ☐ Fails to give statistics on sales/profits
- ☐ Promises 'easy sales'
- ☐ Fails to identify directors or principals
- ☐ Tries to 'trade you up' to a higher fee
- ☐ Says 'act now, it'll cost more later'
- ☐ Promises profits by sub-franchising
- ☐ Has a name similar to a well-known business
- ☐ Promises large income from 'work from home'
- ☐ Demands large 'front end' licence fee
- ☐ Has very short-term contract
- ☐ Provides no data on track record or financial strength
- ☐ Cannot give plans for future development
- ☐ Has vague territories
- ☐ Is ignorant of competition
- ☐ Has incomprehensible contract
- ☐ Is vague about support and training
- ☐ Has weak advertising
- ☐ Is vague about financial obligations for the franchisee
- ☐ Has poor HQ premises
- ☐ Tries to meet in a hotel
- ☐ Is evasive about access to existing franchisees

Fig. 3. A checklist of key questions to ask when gathering information. (Courtesy of Franchise Development Services Ltd).

- what constraints are written into the franchise contract regarding selling your business

- whether the contract has a get-out clause and whether there are any penalties.

The Franchise Magazine has produced an invaluable checklist for prospective franchisees, reproduced in Figure 3.

If you have any doubts regarding the validity of the answers you have received then these can be checked out by speaking with existing franchisees. However, be wary if you are only given a few names to choose from: these may be carefully selected top performers who only speak highly of the franchisor. You should be given the opportunity to select whom you wish to interview from all franchisees in the franchisor's network.

All of the information and advice you have received must eventually be put into perspective. It is you who will be making the financial, personal and emotional commitment to buying a franchised business and it is you who will have to live with the consequences of your actions.

SHORTLISTING THE OPPORTUNITIES

When selling a business, a franchisor will employ a number of persuasive sales techniques to entice you to buy. The effectiveness of these techniques may give rise to a long list of potential opportunities and, in order to compile a suitable shortlist, you need to keep your franchise objectives clearly focused. Although there are no hard and fast rules governing how your list should be composed, it is sensible to begin with no more than half a dozen carefully selected opportunities.

Taking your time

Regardless of how attractive an opportunity appears to be, it is important never to rush any decision, particularly when it may involve your life savings. Buying a franchise is not like buying food or clothes, you will have to live with your decision for a number of years and therefore it is crucial that your decision is based on sound judgement. The key to compiling an ideal list is to be critically honest with yourself. The first stage is to disregard those opportunities in which you have only a passing interest. It is likely that some of the businesses on your list are included because they looked interesting but were really only pursued as a matter of curiosity. Unless you are 100 per cent committed to a business from the outset then it is doubtful you will achieve long-term success.

Eliminating opportunities beyond your financial means
Even after initial examination your list may still be too long, and the next stage is to eliminate those opportunities which you are unable to afford. Even the most appealing and potentially profitable businesses can prove to be beyond your financial reach. Chapter 5, Financing a Franchise, deals with this in greater detail, but no matter how attractive an opportunity appears to be, a bank will not back a business based simply on appearances alone. You must be prepared to accept that even though some businesses may suit your personal objectives, without sufficient finance your ambitions may remain unrealised. On the other hand, it is important not to buy a business simply because it is all you can afford.

One of the fundamental problems with compiling a shortlist of this nature is that until you have fully investigated all of the opportunities you will be unable to determine whether any will be suitable. There is a possibility that none of the businesses on your initial list will prove suitable and, disheartening as it may be, you will have to start the process again from the beginning. Although this is very time consuming, it is far better to spend a few months investigating your options than to spend thousands of pounds on the wrong business.

COMPILING YOUR RESEARCH

Even at this early stage you will probably have amassed a great deal of information which needs to be compiled in a logical sequence. Chapter 4, Choosing the Right Franchise, examines how to collate and analyse information, but at this stage you are only interested in how to compile your research. Your main objective is to ensure that the information you have collected covers all aspects of the business opportunities that you wish to consider in more detail. It is imperative that you have the same detailed information in respect of each individual franchise so that your final comparison of the pros and cons can be completed on a like-for-like basis.

Your research should be compiled in the form of a four-part analysis with the objective of determining the following information:

- what the franchisor says about the opportunity on offer
- what previous and existing franchisees say about the business
- what others say about the franchise
- what your perceptions of the franchise are.

Some of the answers to the above questions will be gleaned from the franchise prospectus but you must remember that this document is a marketing tool for the franchisor and, like most information brochures, has been designed with the sole purpose of inciting you to buy. An objective and critical approach is therefore necessary, combining your own research with that contained in the prospectus. This is examined in more detail in the next chapter.

CASE STUDIES

Joshua visits a franchise exhibition

After taking a well-earned rest and enjoying some quality time with his family, Joshua decides he wants to sell his business and buy another franchise. Before doing so he visits the National Franchise Exhibition for ideas and inspiration. Although he has enjoyed building up his cleaning franchise, he decides that the time is right for a change. Keeping an open mind, it is Joshua's intention to find a business in a completely different sector that will challenge his business skills. However, even with such a variety of businesses, Joshua finds it very difficult to narrow his search. He leaves the exhibition with plenty of information and decides the time is right to put his existing business on the market.

Jake visits a franchise exhibition

Jake has never been to an exhibition of any nature and is pleasantly surprised by the vast amount of opportunities and information on offer. Ideally he is looking for a business based around his electrical experience but he decides to attend the exhibition with an open mind. From the information he has read prior to attending the exhibition Jake is able to gauge which opportunities he has more than a passing interest in. As well as the various company exhibitions, there are several seminars throughout the day covering all aspects of franchising, from what to look for in a business to how to succeed with a franchise.

Charlotte attends a franchise exhibition

Even with all the information available through the internet, Charlotte decides the next stage is to visit a franchise exhibition. Of the hundreds of opportunities on offer at the exhibition there is only one that appeals to Charlotte. The Movie Store presently sells a comprehensive range of movie memorabilia through mail order but has chosen franchising as a means of expanding its business. Over the last 18 months the company has successfully established and managed a number of high street pilot operations and is using the exhibition to officially launch their franchise opportunity. The first franchisees are offered various incentives to join the network, including a reduced franchise fee and discounts on stock.

ACTION POINTS

1. Make an ordered list of sources for your research.

2. Ensure your questions provide all the information you need from the franchisor and their franchisees.

3. Make sure that the final compilation of your research covers every aspect of your potential franchise(s).

4

Choosing the Right Franchise

ATTENDING FRANCHISE EXHIBITIONS

Attending a franchise exhibition should form an integral part of your selection process when choosing a franchise from the many opportunities currently available. Choosing a franchise may seem a simple enough task; however finding the franchise that is *right* for you is considerably more complex. Throughout the UK there are currently four major annual exhibitions – in London, Birmingham, Manchester and Glasgow – all fully backed by the British Franchise Association (BFA).

Figure 4 shows all the important elements for consideration when choosing your franchise.

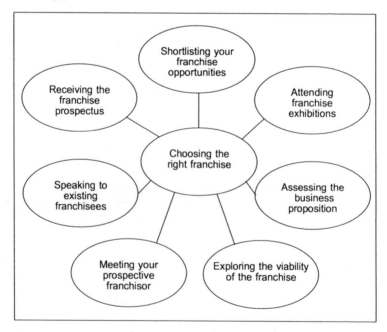

Fig. 4. A scattergram showing the elements of choosing the right franchise.

Assessing the different types of franchise

Franchise exhibitions are like a one-stop shop offering an unprecedented wealth of information from a single source. These exhibitions attract franchisors from a variety of business sectors, giving you the chance to assess and compare a vast number of opportunities all under one roof. The many business propositions available will be as diverse as their respective levels of investment. From a thousand pounds or so to more than a hundred thousand pounds, opportunities will be available to suit every pocket no matter how large or small.

Meeting members of ancillary services

In addition to the franchisors there will be a selection of ancillary services geared towards the franchise industry, and solicitors, lawyers and business consultants will be available to answer any questions you may have. Most of the major banks will be represented, each promoting various schemes and offers to encourage you to bank with them. Your choice of lender does not have to be restricted to where you currently bank. Many building societies also offer business schemes and accounts. and therefore the exhibition will give you the chance to assess and evaluate all the available opportunities. Before committing yourself to any particular banking service you must be sure that they are providing the financial advice and support most suited to your needs and at the most competitive rate.

Seminars

An integral part of any franchise exhibition is its free seminars covering a broad selection of related topics. These seminars, which usually last for about an hour, are well structured and informative and should be included within your itinerary.

Preparing for the exhibition

Obviously not all of the franchises on offer will appeal to you, or be suitable for your circumstances, so to achieve the maximum benefit from an exhibition your visit needs to be planned with forethought and care. If possible try to obtain your exhibition guide a few weeks prior to the show and use this to identify exactly which companies you want to see so that you can strategically plan your time. Many franchise and business orientated magazines offer complimentary tickets in the few months before a show which can help you get the most out of an exhibition.

Listing your priorities

Having decided who you wish to see the next stage is to prioritise
your list. If you contact your prospects early enough you should be
able to make appointments to visit stands and therefore save
yourself a lot of wasted time on the day. Time wasted standing
around could be better utilised working through your list. If you
have any spare time during your visit then take a look at those
companies which caught your attention but did not make your list –
you never know what you may find.

RECEIVING A FRANCHISE PROSPECTUS

An advertisement in a magazine or the design of an exhibition stand
will only create a basic understanding of what a franchise business
entails. After you have shortlisted the opportunities in which you are
interested the next step is to obtain a franchise prospectus. Some
information concerning what a franchise opportunity comprises will
be contained within it. Remember that a franchise prospectus
traditionally only highlights the positive issues, but nevertheless this
important piece of literature forms a vital part of your selection
process.

At a franchise exhibition you can acquire as many prospectuses as
you consider necessary, but if you are responding to an advertisement then your prospectus is likely to arrive through the post. A
vigilant franchisor will follow up every request for information with
a courtesy telephone call to confirm both receipt of their
information and to determine if they can be of any further
assistance. Take care if you are only collecting information at this
stage. There can be nothing more infuriating than receiving
persuasive telephone calls from prospective franchisors if your only
intention at this stage is merely to collect information for later
analysis and perusal.

Assessing the franchisor

A great deal of information about the franchisor will be gained from
the prospectus but do remember to check whether or not the
franchisor is a member of the BFA (see Chapter 3, Gathering
Information). Further knowledge can be gained from interviews
featured in magazines, newspapers or on the radio. When making
your assessment be careful about accepting information at face
value, since persuasive wording can often be used to create an

illusion of a viable opportunity which may not materialise in reality. Always give consideration to the validity of the source – after all, is the franchisor really going to publish, or say, anything derogatory about the business?

MEETING YOUR PROSPECTIVE FRANCHISOR

Having thoroughly examined your written literature and interviews it is time to meet your prospective franchisor for the first time. This is a very important stage of your assessment and will enable you to judge whether what you have learned so far actually presents a true picture of the business on offer. Make sure that you have a comprehensive list of questions ready (see section headed Asking the right questions in Chapter 3), to enable you to fill in any gaps in your investigation.

A franchisor is unlikely to present their opportunity in anything less than a favourable light, but what they are doing can be likened to selling a product. All the features and benefits are highlighted in an attempt to persuade you to buy. However, a good franchisor will draw your attention to any negative aspects that you should be aware of. For example, if you are considering an opportunity to become a milkman then the early morning start is an obvious issue. Nevertheless, despite how comprehensive the franchisor's information may appear, there can be no substitute for finding out exactly what it is like to become a franchisee from somebody who is currently in that position.

SPEAKING TO EXISTING FRANCHISEES

Whether it is written or verbal, the information you receive from a franchisor only forms part of the selection process. A franchisor will be able to illustrate how their franchise concept works but it is only by speaking with existing franchisees that an accurate picture of what it would be like to be associated with a particular company can be achieved.

Getting an unbiased opinion

Despite recommendations from the franchisor, exactly which franchisees you speak to should be left to your own discretion. You may feel more comfortable speaking face to face, as opposed to over the telephone, and therefore the geographical location of both you and your source will influence who you contact. But a good franchisor will have no objection to you contacting anyone throughout their network so that you can gain an unbiased and realistic impression.

Exploring the advantages and disadvantages

The purpose of contacting an existing franchisee should be twofold. Firstly, you need to ascertain that the advantages stated by the franchisor are both achievable and workable concepts. For example, if your franchisor tells you that your business will show a profit after 12 months then will the demand for your product or service enable this to happen? Secondly, you need to discover exactly what the disadvantages are to determine if they outweigh the opportunity itself. For example, you may be expected to work constantly long hours or make additional financial contributions for equipment or stock.

Finding out more

As with franchisors, further experiences of franchisees can be obtained from various media interviews. However once again, do not forget to take account of the reliability of the source. A franchisee may have had an unfortunate experience with the business and therefore have a low opinion of their franchisor or, alternatively, they may be held in high regard by the franchisor and be reluctant to say anything that may be less than complimentary.

EVALUATING A FRANCHISE

Evaluating a franchise is a very comprehensive process and can only follow careful analysis of all the information you have received. Research is one of the primary keys to success and is an invaluable component in the process of evaluating a franchise.

Shortlisting your franchise opportunities

Your research to date should have enabled you to shortlist a number of franchise opportunities which may be from the same industry or from a variety of segments. The important aspect is that these are opportunities in which you are genuinely interested and areas in which you feel competent to undertake and start a business. For example, if you do not have an interest in the motor industry then it is unlikely that your choice will be influenced just because an opportunity in that sector looks viable. The two most important elements of a successful franchise are viability and interest: you will not succeed unless you have both.

Combining your research from both franchisor and franchisees, together with media interviews and reviews from other people, should give you an overall picture of your chosen options on which to base your interpretation of the information in making your evaluation.

Exploring the viability of the franchise

The viability of a franchise is obviously a very important issue. The first step is to analyse the product or service offered in relation to its position within the market place. The franchise may be well established or a relatively new concept, but at some point it must have been tried and tested by a pilot scheme in order to demonstrate its profitability. The market place is continuously changing and a good franchisor will have developed a product or service that is flexible enough to adapt to current and future consumer trends in order to sustain long-term success. A franchise which has been established purely in line with a current craze or fad will only ever achieve short-term success.

Assessing the competition

One aspect of evaluation often overlooked by prospective franchisees is the strength of the competition. How well does your product or service compare with similar ones in the market place in relation to both quality and price? If your business charges are higher than relevant competitors then you must be sure that you are providing a product or service that is comparatively better, and that potential customers will be prepared to pay this price. Some franchisors insist that you adhere to their own pricing structure so it is important to evaluate how this will affect your revenue.

Considering your location

The position of both your exclusive operating territory and your site can greatly affect the viability of a business. A shop selling handmade evening gowns is unlikely to achieve the same level of success in a small town as in a highly populated area.

There are various methods to determine exclusive territory allocation. Some franchisors allocate a set number of postal codes, whilst others allocate by town or county. Much will depend on the nature of your business. This can also influence the position of your site within your territory. For example, the site of a parcel distribution franchise is likely to be positioned central to the area the business covers.

ASSESSING THE BUSINESS PROPOSITION

No single business is ever established without a certain element of risk. Although franchising reduces the risk factor by using tried and tested business formulas, it will not totally eliminate all risk. There are many reports which highlight the unprecedented success rate of the franchise industry but that does not mean that every single franchised business opportunity will succeed. On the contrary, every opportunity needs to be evaluated on its own merits rather than as part of a larger organisation. And the amount of financial investment should not be used as a guide to success. Just because one opportunity costs twice as much as another to purchase it does not necessarily follow that you will make twice as much profit.

Examining start-up costs

The start-up costs of any franchise will obviously vary according to the type of business and where the business is going to be operated from. For example, a van-based distribution business will require less start-up capital than a retail outlet requiring premises. Regardless of the type of business, all start-up costs should be carefully scrutinised and, most importantly, justified. It is important that you understand exactly what you are being asked to pay for before you proceed any further. An apparently viable opportunity can easily become outweighed by large and sometimes unnecessary start-up costs. If you are in any doubt then always seek independent professional advice. The BFA has a list of professional advisers who have been vetted and approved by them who are well versed in all aspects of the franchising concept. *Never* under any circumstances sign anything unless you are 100 per cent sure you know what you are signing for. Chapter 5, Financing a Franchise, examines start-up costs in more detail.

Exploring whether there's a market

When you assess the risk factor of a particular opportunity it is not only the financial risk you need to address. Before proceeding with any venture you need to be certain that a sufficient level of demand exists within the market place. The buying trends of your potential customers need to be considered as well as their number. Fifty thousand potential customers are likely to remain only potential unless they need or can be persuaded to buy your product or service.

Market research is essential whether you are entering an existing market place or creating a new one and will vary according to your particular business. Every market evolves through a continual process of growth, maturity and decline and by examining the position of your business within the current cycle, you can project your expected profitability. Your local library and the internet will be invaluable tools when conducting your research. Libraries regularly purchase economic and statistical government reports which can be used to gauge market trends. In addition, populations of towns and cities can be used to quantify market size. Similarly, an internet search of economic and statistical sites, such as the Office of National Statistics, will provide a number of online reports and links to other related sites.

CASE STUDIES

Joshua finds a new business

Unable to find a suitable franchise, Joshua expands his search to include international companies looking to develop their businesses overseas. An international franchise magazine seems to be advertising the perfect opportunity. A large American corporation is offering a regional franchise which comprises several smaller franchised areas. The business analyses the overheads of large companies and helps to reduce their expenses on a no-win-no-fee basis in exchange for a percentage of savings. Their method of operation will enable Joshua to fully utilise his managerial skills by becoming both franchisor and franchisee. Although this type of business can generate large financial rewards, the risk is significantly higher and Joshua will initially need to make a substantial capital investment for the franchise fee. Most of this fee can be financed through his bank providing he manages to sell his business.

Jake visits franchisors

After analysing all the information he has received, Jake shortlists two opportunities both based in the electrical sector. The first franchise involves undertaking general electrical work on a contract basis and the second is with CheckElec, a home-based franchise which inspects and maintains electrical appliances for both domestic and commercial clients. Jake feels that electrical inspections and maintenance would be the most profitable of the two opportunities and makes an appointment with CheckElec. Jake is impressed with how the franchise operates and decides that this would be a good opportunity to buy providing he can afford the purchase price.

Charlotte finds the perfect franchise

The Movie Store franchise would be the perfect opportunity for Charlotte: not only has she previously been used to dealing with the general public but she also has a passionate interest in the products she would be selling. Charlotte realises that running a business is very different from managing one, but with her determination she knows she can succeed. The Movie Store franchise requires a £30,000 investment which includes the franchise fee, opening stock and working capital. The location and cost of the business premises are arranged by the franchisor. In order to ensure each store carries the same stock, Charlotte would be required to purchase her stock directly from the franchisor.

ACTION POINTS

1. Shortlist the companies you wish to visit at the franchise exhibition.

2. Analyse and evaluate the information gained from franchisors and franchisees and then determine *your* optimum franchise opportunity and location.

3. Make sure that your chosen franchise has a marketable product or service and that there is a sufficient demand.

5

Financing a Franchise

With the exception of a few fortunate individuals, the majority of people buying into a franchise will do so with the help of additional finance. To gain finance you will need to begin with a critical assessment of your franchise opportunity, ascertaining its strengths and weaknesses. This information then needs to be presented in a comprehensible format for submission to your prospective lender. This document is known as a business plan.

PREPARING YOUR BUSINESS PLAN

The purpose of a **business plan** is to present your business proposal in a clear and concise manner. This will give a prospective lender a valuable insight into how the business operates. Any decision to lend money can then be based on sound judgement. There is not sufficient space in this book to describe in detail how to prepare a business plan, (the Further Reading section at the end of this book lists other useful publications), but your business plan should cover the following topics:

- your qualities as a business person
- the nature of the business
- your staff and principal investors
- the operational aspects of the business
- your market and competitors
- financial aspects.

Your qualities as a business person
The plan should be used as an opportunity to introduce yourself to your prospective lender. Remember, the person reading your business plan knows very little about you and probably even less about the business. This is your chance to summarise your educational and professional background and describe your

financial needs, including your personal contribution, for the business. Relevant previous experience needs to be included and an explanation of why you have chosen this particular business.

The nature of the business

In addition to basic information such as business name, address and telephone number, this section will provide a comprehensive overview of the business, describing:

- how it operates
- what your aims and objectives are.

Your objectives should be realistic and achievable and coincide with the information supplied in your financial projections. Bearing in mind that your prospective lender knows very little about your business, never be afraid to state the obvious and always provide as much information as possible. Beware of using technical jargon. It may be unnecessary and only serve to confuse the reader.

Your staff and principal investors

These are the key people involved with the business and include both employees and investors. You don't need to list every employee by name, but do give the names and attributes of your key staff members and briefly summarise their role within your business. This section should also include a contingency plan covering how the business will operate in your absence. Your principal investors need to be listed at this stage with a summary describing the conditions governing the terms of their investment.

The operational aspects of the business

This is the nuts and bolts of the business: how the business will operate is as important as what you will be selling. Your prospective financier needs to know that you have considered the organisational structure of the business, including general business administration such as invoicing and accountancy. This section should focus on your methods for attracting and retaining customers and detail your contingency plans for dealing with customer disputes. The constraints imposed by the franchisor governing your territory will affect how the business operates and should be included at this stage.

Your market and competitors

Your market and competitors form one of the most important

aspects of your business plan. Just knowing that you have a product to sell or a service to provide will not be sufficient. You need to examine your position fully within the market place by analysing the strengths and weaknesses of the competition in relation to your own competitive edge.

Financial aspects

Determining how much finance you need is very difficult to predict accurately but it is extremely important to get it right. Borrowing too much money will mean higher repayments, whilst not borrowing enough could prove to be fatal. A carefully compiled cash flow forecast will illustrate how much money you need, when you need it, when you can repay it and which method of finance will be most suited to your business. This section should include evidence of assets you are prepared to offer as security for the loan.

Submitting your business plan

Your business plan should be sent to your prospective lender prior to your initial meeting. This will enable an in-depth assessment of your proposal to be made and will highlight any points that may require further clarification. Figure 5 shows a sample letter which may be sent when submitting your business plan.

It is essential that you are familiar with the contents of your plan and are able to convey this information confidently to a third party. Presenting your business plan to a friend or colleague is an excellent way to help determine your best approach. The more you know about your plan the more impressed your prospective lender will be. However, no matter how impressive or well-presented a business plan is, if the franchise opportunity itself is not viable, then it is very unlikely that your proposal will be successful.

ASSESSING YOUR START-UP COSTS

There is no set formula for determining the cost of taking up a franchise. Each system will differ according to the nature of the business and the location and size of your premises. Investment levels may be as low as £5,000 for a home-based business or as much as £500,000 for a branded fast-food restaurant. However, regardless of the business size there are common areas of expenditure characteristic in most franchises such as:

55 New Street, Weytown, Dorset DT12 3ER
Tel: 01305 231094

1 July 20XX

Mr R Saunders
The Manager
Euro Bank
10 The High Street
Weytown
Dorset
DT12 4SA

Dear Mr. Saunders

Check-Elec Franchise
Business Plan

Further to my telephone conversation I am pleased to confirm
my meeting with you on 9 July 20XX. As agreed, I am enclosing
a copy of my business plan for my proposed venture.

The initial cost of buying into my franchise will be £12,000,
comprising £8000 for the franchise fee and £4000 to finance my
working capital. I have £7000 of my own funds and am hoping to
raise the remaining £5000 with the help of your bank.

I hope I have included all the relevant information to support my
application. However should you require any further details prior
to our meeting, then please do not hesitate to contact me. In the
meantime I look forward to meeting you at 2.15 p.m. on 9 July.

Yours sincerely

Jake Connor

Fig. 5. A specimen letter to a potential source of finance.

- initial and ongoing franchise fees
- premises
- fixed assets
- working capital
- advertising.

Initial and ongoing franchise fees

The franchise fee is a one-off fee to cover the franchisor's costs in setting you up in business. Ongoing fees payable by the franchisee will be for continued services provided by the franchisor. These fees are calculated in various ways according to the type of business and are examined in more detail in Chapter 6, Buying a Franchise.

Premises

The cost of premises will vary considerably and will be dependent on a number of factors including:

- the size of the business
- the nature of the business
- the location of the business
- whether the premises are to be bought, leased or rented.

If the premises are to be leased then you need to ensure that your franchise agreement will not terminate part-way through your lease period. Some franchisors overcome this by becoming the principal leaseholder and then granting franchisees a sub-lease. However, before signing any documents it is imperative to read the small print and be certain that you fully understand the implications.

Fixed assets

It is likely your business will require a certain amount of fixed assets, such as equipment and possibly one or more vehicles. When considering the purchase of equipment you should make provision for updating and modernisation. The franchisor may stipulate that certain types of machinery or equipment have to be used and installed within a defined period of time. This may result in high expenditure. You will need to determine whether it will be best to buy outright or use one of the finance options summarised below.

Finance lease

The legal ownership of the asset is retained by the finance company, and you pay a rental to use the asset for an agreed period. At the end of the lease you have the option either to extend the lease or to sell the asset on behalf of the finance company and retain a proportion of the sale proceeds.

Operating lease
As with a finance lease legal ownership is retained by the finance company but at the end of the agreed period the asset is returned. The asset will not appear on the balance sheet but the monthly rentals are offset against taxable income.

Contract hire
This is very similar to an operating lease but usually includes additional services such as maintenance and servicing. The tax position is the same as an operating lease.

Hire purchase
After making the final payment this option enables you to own the asset. From a tax point of view, the asset is regarded as yours from the beginning and all writing down allowances can be offset against taxable income.

Lease purchase
From a tax point of view the asset is treated in the same manner as hire purchase. However, unlike hire purchase a final lump-sum payment prior to ownership is deferred until the end of the agreement. This reduces the monthly repayments which in turn helps with cash flow.

Working capital
As with any new business, there will be periods when expenses have to be met regardless of whether you have been paid by your customers. Working capital is the term used to describe the money required to finance the day-to-day running of the business.

Advertising
The cost of advertising may be included in your franchise fee, met by the franchisor or shown as an additional expense. It is important to ensure that *you* benefit from local advertising and are not contributing only towards promoting the network as a whole or the sale of franchises. However, national advertising may be necessary if the franchise is relatively new which, in turn, will benefit individual franchisees. Your franchise agreement should include details of who pays for what.

RAISING CAPITAL

Assessing your personal finances

Whether it is for the initial purchase or for future development plans, most businesses will require some form of external finance at some stage. Before contemplating the purchase of a franchise you will need to ascertain exactly how much money you can borrow and from whom. The first stage is to determine how much money you can invest in the business. You may not have a great deal of savings but you may have assets such as property that can either be converted into cash or used as security for your loan. It is important to be completely honest with both yourself and your prospective lender. Prior to loaning you money, your lender will need to determine if the element of risk is actually worth taking. He will also want to be certain of your ability to meet your loan repayments.

Borrowing from a bank

The major banks which previously shunned the franchise industry now recognise franchising as a safer way of establishing a new business. In fact, the banks now operate separate franchise departments and even produce a range of literature specifically geared towards franchising.

The advantage of having a specialised franchise department is that banks are able to reach universal decisions regarding what constitutes a viable franchise opportunity. This means that local branch managers are able to base their decision to authorise or decline franchise loan applications on a thorough risk assessment by having access to all of the relevant information. This is further enhanced by their knowledge and expertise of both local market trends and, more importantly, of the loan applicant themselves.

Satisfying your franchisor

Even if you manage successfully to borrow the total cost of buying a franchise, a franchisor will not necessarily consider you as a prospective franchisee. Having to borrow all or nearly all of your investment will leave you financially vulnerable in the event of unforeseen expenses. It is unusual for a franchisor to offer finance directly to their franchisees. The issue of finance should be completely eliminated from the relationship between franchisor and franchisee. There are too many conflicts of interest for any finance scheme to be successfully operated. For example, if you are unable to meet a loan repayment then the franchisor may suspend your supply of products which would be detrimental to both parties.

Understanding independent finance schemes

A franchisor may have established an independent finance scheme through a bank and will be able to provide you with contact details. You will then be dealing with the bank and not the franchisor. As a cautionary note, remember that just because a bank operates a finance scheme it does not mean they are endorsing or recommending the potential success of a particular opportunity. You should still fully investigate the franchise opportunity and reach your own conclusions. Besides, the information you have collated will be up to date and may portray a different picture of the franchisor from when the bank made their appraisal.

Comparing individual lenders

Although each loan proposal is judged on its own merit, banks would not previously lend any more than 50 per cent of the total purchase price. However, with a well-established franchise banks will often increase this ratio to 70 per cent of the total purchase price. The golden rule when raising finance is always to shop around and compare the various schemes available. Banks operate in a very competitive market and constantly offer various incentives to obtain and retain your business, such as free banking for an introductory period or preferential interest rates. Your local branch manager will be able to recommend which method of borrowing will be best suited to your individual needs.

LOCATING SOURCES OF FINANCE

According to the latest Nat West/BFA Franchise Survey 52 per cent of all new franchisees needed to borrow money to set up in business. Banks have emerged as the most important source of finance and account for 76 per cent of franchisee borrowing. Each of the five main lending banks produce their own free business start-up guides which contain a wealth of information, practical advice and some have even developed their own business planning computer software. In addition, the banks have gone one stage further and produced supplementary guides written specifically for the franchise sector. These guides are available either from the local branches or by contacting the banks direct at the following addresses:

Barclays Bank plc, Franchise Department, PO Box 120, Longwood Close, Westwood Business Park, Coventry CV4 8JN. Tel: (02476) 534433

HSBC, Franchise Unit, 10 Lower Thames Street, London EC3R 6AE. Tel: (0207) 260 6783

Lloyds TSB Bank plc, Retail Banking UKRB, PO Box 112, Canon's Way, Bristol BS99 7LB. Tel: (0117) 943 3410

National Westminster Bank plc, Retail Banking Services, Franchise Section, Level 10 Drapers Gardens, 12 Throgmorton Avenue, London EC2N 2DL. Tel: (0207) 920 5966

The Royal Bank of Scotland plc, Franchise and Licensing Department, PO Box 31, 42 St Andrew's Square, Edinburgh EH2 2YE. Tel: (0131) 523 2178

Lending options

As previously mentioned, each bank will offer a different range of loan and banking options depending on your individual criteria. Most of the banks should be able to provide a combination of the following lending options:

- franchise loans
- capital repayment holiday
- overdraft
- leasing
- Small Firms Loan Guarantee Scheme (LGS)
- factoring.

Franchise loans

These can be used to finance the cost of the franchise or to develop the business at a later date. Some banks impose minimum and maximum amounts but can usually offer a choice of fixed, variable or capped interest rates over a mutually agreed repayment period.

Capital repayment holiday

This option is designed to ease cash flow during the early stages of the business and is particularly useful for businesses which will not initially generate any surplus revenue but will be able to meet larger repayments at a later date.

Overdraft

This is the most popular and cost-effective method of financing short-term borrowing such as working capital. Periodic arrangement fees are payable and interest is charged on outstanding balances. Overdrafts are technically repayable on demand and therefore are not suitable to finance long-term expenses such as fixed assets.

Leasing

This option is mainly used to finance fixed assets such as plant, equipment and vehicles without having to find the full cost at the outset. Fixed monthly payments are made on leases which means budgeting is made simple and working capital is fully utilised within the business. The various types of lease options have already been examined under the heading, Assessing your start-up costs.

Small Firms Loan Guarantee Scheme (LGS)

This government-backed scheme enables small independent businesses to obtain finance which would have otherwise been unavailable due to their lack of loan security. Under the scheme the government stand as a guarantor for a proportion of your loan up to £100,000 for new businesses or £250,000 for businesses with a two-year trading history. You will be expected to pay an insurance premium to the government which is currently 0.5 per cent of the government's risk. The loan is repayable over two to ten years with the option of a possible two year capital repayment holiday. A fixed interest is charged by the bank just above the base rate.

Factoring

Franchises who invoice business customers for their services can use a factoring company to receive almost immediately 80 per cent of the cash due to them. This helps business cash flow by releasing money tied up in unpaid invoices. Companies are then free to concentrate on the core aspects of building up the business and are totally safeguarded against bad debts. Depending on the size and turnover of the business, a factoring company will retain between 0.5 and 3.5 per cent of the remaining 20 per cent of debts as a handling charge. The Association of British Factors can provide a full list of its members: contact them at 1 Northumberland Avenue, London WC2N 5BW, Tel: (0207) 930 9112.

This is by no means an exhaustive list as this book concentrates on the more traditional sources and methods of finance available through the high street banks. Your own research will uncover additional options and schemes for you to consider. Remember, it is unlikely that one solitary method of finance will completely satisfy your financial needs. A financial adviser able to devise a tailor-made 'package' that will utilise every penny within your business in the most cost-effective way will be worth their weight in gold.

ASSESSING YOUR POTENTIAL INCOME

In a franchised network, all units must operate in accordance with a predefined formula and each business must conform to identical business practices. However, in spite of operational similarities each business within a franchised network is unique in respect of its earning potential. The profitability of a franchised business will vary according to a number of integrated variables including:

- **The location of your business in relation to the products you sell or services you provide**

Businesses in highly populated areas should theoretically generate a larger turnover than those in smaller towns. However, this must be compared with the differences in the cost of operating a business in each of the two areas.

- **Local market prices**

If your selling prices are controlled by your franchisor then you must consider the effect this will have on your turnover. Will your customers be prepared to pay your prices if similar products or services are available locally at a cheaper cost?

- **The demand for your product or service**

You must be sure that there will be a sufficient demand for your business in order to operate at a profit. Just because a particular franchise is successful in one part of the country it does not necessarily follow that the same level of success can be replicated in your area.

- **The level of local competition**

The strength of your immediate competitors must be evaluated against the effect this will have on your business. If similar products or services are locally available then how – and how easily – will you attract customers away from the competition?

A complete assessment of your potential income can only be achieved by carefully scrutinising every expense against your estimated turnover. The majority of these figures can be calculated and verified by cross-referencing information from your franchisor, existing franchisees and what you know about local market prices. The importance of getting these projections as accurate as possible cannot be stressed enough. They are used by the bank to evaluate your ability to make loan repayments and by you to monitor your progress and determine your potential income.

Seeking independent advice

The importance of seeking independent professional advice must also be stressed. The payment of franchise fees and the purchase of assets are areas where you can benefit enormously from sound financial advice. Legal advice should also be sought, particularly in respect of rental and lease agreements. This type of professional advice and guidance is essential at this stage if you are going to make a true assessment of your potential income.

CASE STUDIES
Joshua finds a buyer

Joshua decides that a combination of local and national advertising will be the most effective way to find a buyer. This strategy proves successful and a number of potentially suitable buyers are shortlisted. As a provision of his franchise agreement, the new franchisee must be approved by Clean and Gleam prior to the business being sold. Joshua is given the opportunity to interview his potential buyers initially before they receive the official seal of approval from Clean and Gleam. Between both parties a shortlist of six suitable purchasers is compiled, subject to each being able to meet the purchase price. Following an in-depth interview with Clean and Gleam a suitable buyer is given the opportunity to buy the business.

Jake raises the finance

Before committing himself to buying the franchise Jake first needs to raise £12,000. The franchise fee will cost £8000 and the remaining £4000 will finance working capital during the initial trading period. Jake has £7000 in savings and intends to raise the remaining £5000 from his bank. His first task is to prepare a business plan which, with the help of the franchisor and existing franchisees, proves to be simpler than he first envisaged. The bank manager is able to see the potential of the franchise and, as the loan will be less than Jake's contribution, the loan is approved.

Charlotte approaches the bank

Charlotte decides to pursue the Movie Store franchise and begins to compile a business plan before she approaches the bank for a loan. Her projections are based on a combination of facts and figures supplied by the franchisor and what she already knows about the industry. Charlotte is convinced that she will succeed and is prepared to put her entire savings into the business and, if necessary, use her house as security. With her business plan completed Charlotte approaches the bank intending to raise the remaining £15,000.

ACTION POINTS

1. Make sure that your business plan contains all the relevant information in a concise form.

2. Make a true assessment of your start-up costs.

3. Decide which type of finance is most suitable for your business.

6

Buying a Franchise

The preceding chapters have examined the elements which together comprise a viable franchise opportunity. It is only now, after you have gathered, analysed and evaluated your research, that you will be in a position to contemplate buying a franchise. Your research will have highlighted potential businesses – probably including both new and established franchises – and eliminated those which are unsuitable. Having decided that franchising is the right type of business for you the next step is to choose between a new and an existing franchise.

SETTING UP A NEW FRANCHISE

Setting up a new franchise can be both exciting and rewarding. Your efforts will be directly contributing towards the overall development of the franchised system. Although the risks of a franchised business are significantly lower than an independent new venture the risks are, nevertheless, still evident. A new franchise is essentially a new business in an unproven market. Therefore, it is necessary to undertake a more extensive level of research than with an established franchise.

Testing the franchised system

The system must be fully pilot-tested by the franchisor prior to being marketed. This can take up to two years as the commercial viability of the business needs to be validated in a variety of locations and under a multitude of market constraints. A profitable pilot operation is not a guarantee that the same degree of success can be easily replicated. When contemplating a new franchise you need to look beyond the information supplied by the franchisor. For example, the financial projections will be based on an average of the sales and expenses of the pilot operations. The costs of your franchise may vary considerably depending on local conditions.

Evaluating a new franchise

A new franchise is very difficult to evaluate fully as most of the important information will not yet be available. However, further research of the franchisor and their operational methods is necessary before committing yourself to a particular opportunity. Your analysis will need to examine the following areas which can adversely affect the success of your franchise:

- franchisee recruiting methods
- financial resources
- organisational structure.

Franchisee recruiting methods
The methods used to recruit new franchisees will directly affect the overall success of the network. This is particularly evident with new franchises which will often inadvertently accept unsuitable applicants. This generally occurs when the franchisor is either anxious to recoup some of their expenses quickly, or has not fully identified the skills necessary to operate a particular franchise.

Financial resources
It can take a number of years before a franchisor achieves any degree of profitability, so it is essential to determine the extent of the franchisor's financial resources and commitment. This will ensure the business is able to survive during its early stages of development. Some businesses naively believe that franchising will solve their financial problems when in reality it will only add to them. Businesses that have turned to franchising for this reason should be avoided at all costs.

Organisational structure

The organisational structure of the franchise is of equal importance as the opportunity itself. The successful organisation of any franchised business is dependent on a good working relationship between the franchisor and franchisee. According to the service being provided, or the product being sold, different levels of responsibility will be required from the franchisee. In line with this a reliable and accessible support system must be provided by the franchisor. A typical organisational structure is set out in Figure 6.

As with any business, it takes time and experience to establish a working harmony. Your franchisor will be subject to making mistakes just like any other business owner. A poorly researched and

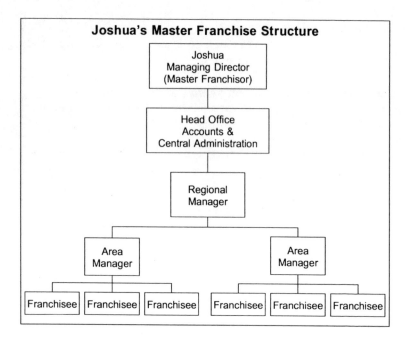

Fig. 6. An organisational chart.

weak structure can be detrimental to the business even if a ready-made market exists. A well-structured franchise will not guarantee success but it will improve your chances of achieving it. You must be able to conclude that the franchisor is fully equipped to operate the business successfully.

TAKING OVER AN EXISTING FRANCHISE

Purchasing an existing franchise will involve the introduction of a third party, the vendor. Although you are buying from the vendor and not directly from the franchisor, you still need to meet the franchisor's criteria. Existing franchises will require a higher level of investment as the business is established and has a proven value. However, unlike purchasing a new franchise direct from the franchisor, the purchase price can generally be negotiated with the vendor. There will be conditions governing the sale which will be described in the vendor's franchise agreement. It is a common requirement for the vendor to initially offer the business to the franchisor as they have contributed towards the development of the franchise.

Both new and existing franchises involve equal amounts of research, analysis and evaluation. Although there are fewer risks with an existing franchise, this does not mean the business has an improved chance of succeeding. On the contrary, the present franchisee could be selling because they are unable to make the business work.

Checking past performance

Existing franchises have the advantage of their own previous trading history which enables your research to be verified with actual facts and figures. This is in complete contrast to a new franchise that is dependent on the franchisor's calculations of start-up costs and financial projections.

It is important to ascertain why the franchise is being offered for sale. There may be a perfectly legitimate reason, such as the vendor no longer enjoys the work or his personal circumstances may have altered. Alternatively, it may be that the business is not capable of producing and sustaining an acceptable profit level. This may be due to unreasonable constraints imposed by the franchisor or due to the fact that the business is not viable in its particular location.

The reason given for sale should be verified and not automatically accepted on face value. Caution does not cost anything but can save a lot of time and money in the long run.

Examining previous accounts

Depending on when the franchise was established, you should ideally have access to at least three years' accounts. Anything less is unlikely to reflect accurately how the business has progressed. These figures can then be used to forecast future performance based on previous trading history. The validity of the financial accounts will depend on the type of business and their intended purpose. For example, a limited company only needs to present minimal financial information to Companies House.

A full analysis of the business can only be determined by viewing the financial accounts in conjunction with detailed management accounts. Sole trader and partnership year-end accounts do not need to be audited but they are used to assess tax liability. They can often reflect reduced profits which will reduce the amount of tax payable. When you are confident of the accuracy of the accounts you can build up a more accurate picture of how the business has progressed.

DEFINING YOUR LOCATION

Ascertaining your optimum location

Having decided which franchise to buy you must be certain that the business will work in your area. The optimum location of your business is completely dependent on the nature of the franchise. For example, a business that relies on passing trade, such as a retail outlet, will need a prime town centre position. Conversely location will not be as important to a business that visits its customers, such as carpet cleaners or home repairs. In this case an out-of-town base may be cost effective, provided it is central to your main sales area. Your initial research will have already highlighted the general location issues that need to be addressed. Now your research needs to focus on location issues specific to your business.

Finding suitable premises

Your franchise agreement will state who decides where to locate the business, you or the franchisor. The location of a brand-named franchise, particularly in the retail sector, is crucial to its success. Franchisors of these businesses have established precise location requirements as a result of continuous market research. In these cases, it is common for franchisors to find premises and control the freehold or lease. This will not affect the working relationship between you and the franchisor but problems can arise when the agreement expires. The franchisor can reclaim the premises, which means you will either have to relocate the business or decide not to renew your agreement. In this event you will be compensated in accordance with the terms of your franchise agreement. If you have made improvements to the premises, the amount of compensation can be difficult to calculate accurately.

Taking over existing premises

If you are taking over an existing business then your location may already be predetermined. The existing franchisee may be renting premises which are available to you as the successor, but may have an individually agreed rental which is not transferable. The landlord may be happy to continue letting the premises but will quite possibly want to review the rental agreement.

The same caution needs to be exercised when taking over an existing lease agreement. Unless you are buying a freehold property as part of the business, you will need to examine the conditions of the present lease agreement. For example, the terms of the lease may hold you to the premises for a number of years. This will prevent you from relocating to a more commercially viable site as your business expands or market trends alter.

UNDERSTANDING THE FRANCHISE FEE

The franchise fee comprises all money payable to the franchisor and is essentially the purchase price of the business. It will include the cost of setting up the business but will exclude additional expenses such as working capital. The franchise fee can be separated into three main areas:

- the initial fee
- ongoing management service fees
- royalty fees.

The initial fee
This is a one-off payment imposed by the franchisor to procure your right to operate the franchised system. The fee will partially reimburse the franchisor's costs for setting you up in business and will include your initial training, the provision of operating manuals, marketing, opening stock and equipment. Never be afraid to ask for a breakdown illustrating how this fee is both calculated and allocated.

The franchise fee must be relative to the rest of your start-up costs and should not include a large profit for the franchisor. The franchisor's profits should be generated through ongoing fees in the form of justifiable royalties. However, a proportion of the fee will be used by the franchisor to help finance costs such as franchisee recruitment and developing the franchise system. These are perfectly justified as they will benefit the network as a whole.

Ongoing management service fees
These are regularly paid to the franchisor on either a weekly or a monthly basis. The fees are in return for the continued management services provided by the franchisor such as advice, training and support. The methods used to calculate and collect fees will vary between franchised businesses. Generally, one of the following methods or a combination of both will be used:

- a percentage of your gross turnover less any VAT
- a mark-up on stock supplied by the franchisor.

As mentioned in Chapter 1, a conflict sometimes occurs when ongoing fees are calculated as a percentage of turnover. A franchisor may automatically increase selling prices, thereby increasing turnover. This in turn will increase the fees due from the franchisee. To an individual franchise this may prove detrimental if the customer base within that particular area cannot withstand the price increase. The franchisee's preferred option may be to reduce overheads and improve efficiency in order to become more cost effective and profitable.

Royalty fees

These are often confused with management fees as both are payable to the franchisor using similar methods of calculation. However, both fees are separate entities which serve different purposes. Management fees paid cover the services provided by the franchisor whereas royalty fees are in respect of the legal right to use the franchisor's brand name.

Assessing fees

All fees charged by the franchisor must be both fair and justified but only you are in a position to determine if they are. As a rule you should be wary of front-loaded franchises with high initial fees and relatively low royalties. A low royalty may mean that your franchisor derives their profits from either large initial fees or a high mark-up on goods or services provided. This is where independent advice from an accountant or business adviser will prove to be invaluable, as discussed in the last chapter.

The deposit

At the outset of agreeing to purchase a franchise you will be required to pay a deposit to your franchisor's solicitor. The exact sum of the deposit will vary between businesses but is usually calculated at between 5 and 10 per cent of the total purchase price. The payment of the deposit is discussed in more detail later in the chapter under the section covering the purchase agreement.

MEETING THE FRANCHISOR

The penultimate stage when purchasing a franchise is meeting your intended franchisor. This will serve as an introduction from the perspective of both parties. Just as your franchisor will be evaluating you as a potential franchisee you will be evaluating them as a potential franchisor. To get the most from your meeting you need to spend some time preparing for it. Begin by reading through your research information and note any issues that need to be clarified.

The principal objective of the meeting should be for the franchisor and the franchisee to assess each other's qualities, as well as the franchise agreement. After all, a franchisor will not make an opportunity available until they are confident of your ability to succeed as a franchisee.

Signing a confidentiality agreement

During, or shortly before, the meeting you may be required to sign a **confidentiality agreement**. This is a short simple document, an example of which is shown in Figure 7. It confirms your agreement not to disclose or use any of the information you have been given concerning the operating methods or practices of the franchisor. It is essentially a safeguard for the franchisor against a third party replicating the business without consent. The existence of a confidentiality agreement is also your reassurance that the information you have paid for is not freely available to others.

DECIDING TO BUY

Assessing the franchise

By the end of the meeting you will finally have access to all the information your franchisor has to offer. This will be your first opportunity to assess the opportunity fully and decide whether or not to enter into a franchised business. You will not be expected to make an immediate decision and indeed you may have to wait until the franchisor has vetted other potential purchasers. This delay is an ideal opportunity to take time to review the situation. Make sure that your initial research concurs with the new information you have gained from your meeting. If there are any areas of conflict then these points need further investigation to ensure you have a true picture.

Benefiting from new information

With the benefit of your new information a detailed assessment of the franchise can be made. This is where the independent professional advice of an accountant or bank manager can prove invaluable. As part of your analysis you must determine if the advantages of a franchised business outweigh the constraints imposed by the franchisor. Before proceeding with your purchase you should give careful consideration to the advantages and

CONFIDENTIALITY AGREEMENT
BETWEEN
Movie Store Holdings Limited (disclosing party)
and
Charlotte Beaumont (receiving party)

INTRODUCTION

WHEREAS, the disclosing party has claim to certain confidential information; and WHEREAS, in connection with the evaluation of a franchise opportunity confidential information may become available to the receiving party. WHEREAS, the disclosing party desires to prevent the unauthorised use and disclosure of such information, the parties agree as follows:

1. Confidential Information

1.1 Under the terms of this agreement confidential information shall mean trade secrets, development plans, operating methods, business records, client lists and all other information which may be disclosed in accordance with this agreement and is not generally available to the public.

2. Obligations of the disclosing party

2.1 To make available to the receiving party or grant access to, any and all confidential information considered necessary to fully evaluate the franchise opportunity presented by the disclosing party.

3. Obligations of the receiving party

3.1 To hold and protect all confidential information in confidence and not to publish, broadcast or use, any confidential information made available to them by the disclosing party.

3.2 Upon termination of the business relationship or at the written request of the disclosing party, all records and materials pertaining to the confidential information must be promptly returned to the disclosing party.

3.3 To accept that no right to the confidential information is intended, implied or shall exist.

3.4 To reimburse the disclosing party for any losses, claims, damages, or expenses incurred or suffered as a result of receiving party's breach of this agreement.

4. Exceptions

4.1 Any information that is characterised as confidential shall cease to be on the date when, through no fault of omission of the receiving party, such information becomes disclosed in published literature or otherwise generally available to the industry or the public.

This confidentiality agreement is entered into on 27 May 20XX.

SIGNED: _____   SIGNED: _____
                                                          (Movie Store Holdings Ltd)

NAME: Charlotte Beaumont   NAME: Robert Anderson

Fig. 7. A sample confidentiality agreement.

disadvantages of franchising as discussed in Chapter 1, Defining Franchising.

THE PURCHASE AGREEMENT

A franchise opportunity will only be made available after the franchisor has given careful consideration to all prospective purchasers. The franchisor needs to determine that a successful working relationship can be established that will be commercially beneficial to both parties. Only then will the opportunity be offered to a particular purchaser.

Understanding the conditions of purchase

When agreeing to buy a franchise the first stage to be encountered is the purchase agreement. This short document is issued by the franchisor to set out the conditions of purchase between both parties. Although the precise contents will vary between businesses, essentially each agreement is designed to serve the same purpose. You will be able to purchase the franchise subject to certain criteria being met on both sides.

The purchase agreement

A **purchase agreement** (sometimes called an option agreement) is used by the franchisor to sell a franchised territory and by the purchaser to secure one. If the business is already established, then the agreement will state that subject to reading and approving the franchise agreement within a short specified time, you will purchase the existing business and enter into a legally binding franchise contract. However, for a new franchise unable to start trading immediately, then the agreement will serve a slightly different purpose. An example would be when a trading site needs to be acquired and approved. As already discussed, the responsibility for finding premises will usually rest with the franchisor as they understand what a suitable operating site should comprise. In this case, the agreement would state that subject to suitable premises being found and your acceptance of the franchise agreement you will purchase the business.

Signing your purchase agreement

The importance of a purchase agreement cannot be stressed enough. It is a legally binding document under which you and the franchisor are obligated towards one another. Make sure you understand what you are signing and only sign if you are prepared to accept the full implications of its contents and consequences.

Securing your franchise

Irrespective of whether you are setting up a new franchise, or taking over an existing one, a deposit will be required by the franchisor as part of the initial franchise fee. The amount and terms of this deposit will vary according to individual businesses (see page 72).

If you are purchasing a new franchise the deposit represents your interest in buying the business and is your franchisor's authority to begin looking for a suitable and commercially viable trading site. In addition to this your franchisor will also determine whether planning permission or any other applications are needed before you can start trading. After paying your deposit both you and the franchisor will have a specified time frame, usually a year, to find a suitable site and commence trading. Your deposit will be returned if the franchisor is unable to locate suitable premises within this period. However, if during this time you change your mind or reject a potentially suitable operating site then your deposit will be withheld by your franchisor. In addition you may be liable for other expenses such as lease payments, stock, equipment and possibly compensation to your franchisor.

In the case of an existing franchise the deposit still represents your interest in buying the business. The time frame will usually be a much shorter period allowing time for the details of the sale to be finalised and the legal procedures to be completed. The deposit will still be subject to forfeiture if you do not go ahead with the purchase.

CASE STUDIES

Joshua's buyer exchanges contracts

With the purchase details agreed, Joshua, Clean and Gleam and the new buyer are all in a position finally to exchange contracts. With the purchase of an existing franchise, two separate agreements need to be drawn up. The first is an acquisition agreement between Joshua and the new buyer. This document details the contents of the sale, including all assets. The second document is a franchise agreement between the new buyer and Clean and Gleam which provides details of their obligations towards one another. The contents of the documents are accepted by all three parties which means Joshua is able to finance his new business.

Jake decides to buy a franchise

With the finance agreed Jake has a second meeting with CheckElec and is taken step-by-step through the franchise agreement. The concept of CheckElec is simple: the franchisor arranges initial electrical inspections at homes and business premises. The franchisee undertakes a full electrical inspection and reports any faults that are found. The client then chooses either to have any work completed for a set price or agrees to regular inspections at reduced rates. Regular inspections provide CheckElec with a large proportion of repeat business from satisfied clients. Jake is impressed with both the professional approach of CheckElec and their devotion to maintaining high levels of customer satisfaction. After giving the opportunity considerable thought, Jake decides to buy a CheckElec franchise.

Charlotte signs a purchase agreement

Having successfully arranged her finance with the bank Charlotte meets her prospective franchisor to sign her purchase agreement. Charlotte's franchisor is responsible for finding suitable premises for her. The purchase agreement is a legally binding document and having consulted her solicitor Charlotte signs and pays her initial deposit. Subject to suitable premises being found and her acceptance of the franchise agreement, Charlotte has agreed to purchase the business. If the franchisor is unable to find appropriate premises in the specified time then Charlotte's deposit will be returned to her. Correspondingly if Charlotte were to reject a potential site or change her mind then her deposit will be withheld by her franchisor.

ACTION POINTS

1. Be sure that the franchise is right for you.

2. Make sure that you fully understand the purchase agreement and the calculation of the deposit.

3. Be sure that you are able to work under the controls and regulations of the franchisor.

4. Take professional or legal advice if necessary to make sure that you understand fully what you are agreeing to.

7

Understanding the Franchise Agreement

RECOGNISING KEY POINTS AND CLAUSES OF THE FRANCHISE AGREEMENT

As with a purchase agreement, the precise layout and wording of a **franchise agreement** will vary according to the nature of the business and the operational practices of the franchisor. Although the content of each agreement will be unique there are several universal factors apparent in all franchise contracts. These have been accepted by the franchise community as the elements necessary to constitute a comprehensive franchise agreement.

The key points and clauses of the agreement should cover the following areas in sufficient detail to ensure no ambiguity exists between franchisor and franchisee:

* the intellectual property of the franchisor
* rights granted to the franchisee
* period of contract
* obligations
* operational controls
* sale of the business
* death of the franchisee
* arbitration
* termination.

The intellectual property of the franchisor
This is covered by a series of clauses which provide details of what the franchisor owns in terms of copyright material, trade marks, trade names, and operating methods.

Rights granted to the franchisee
These give the franchisee a legal authority to use the franchisor's intellectual property within a specified territory. Territorial rights are relatively simple to define either by map or postal code allocation. However, they can be notoriously difficult to enforce because

neighbouring franchisees cannot be legally prevented from trading in your area even though the franchisor prohibits their presence.

Period of contract
The average length of a franchise contract is between five and seven years. At the end of the initial period you should be given an option to renew the franchise for a similar, or extended, period. Take care with franchise agreements which do not have an automatic right of renewal. Agreements which have a short initial period and demand ongoing renewal fees should also be treated with caution. This topic is covered in more detail in Chapter 6, Buying a Franchise.

Obligations
Obligations refer to the initial and continuing obligations each party has to the other. This covers the initial services provided by the franchisor to enable your business to commence trading, such as the provision of training and equipment. The franchisor's continual obligations include improving methods, the development of new products or services, marketing and advertising, monitoring and maintaining standards, profitability and performance. Your initial and continuing obligations will include agreeing to finance and run the business in accordance with the franchisor's operational controls.

Operational controls
Operational controls stipulate the precise methods to which each franchisee must adhere. This will ensure that uniform operational standards are maintained throughout the entire franchised network. The agreement will often be cross-referenced with the operational manual, although at this stage you may not have seen it.

The franchise agreement is used to describe the franchisor's controls and the operational manual will detail the methods used to achieve them. Relocation clauses should be regarded with extreme caution. Under certain conditions such as the need for expansion, the franchisor may insist the business be moved to alternative premises. This may result in the choice of a new location or the loss of your franchise.

Sale of the business
This details the controls imposed by the franchisor governing who can buy your franchise. A franchisor will need to determine if your potential purchaser meets the necessary criteria to succeed as a franchisee. The franchisor was selective when initially appointing

franchisees and will therefore insist on being equally selective when an established business is sold.

Death of the franchisee

In the event of anything happening to you, this clause will ensure that the franchisor will offer assistance to protect your business as a saleable asset. The business can then either be sold on your behalf or taken over by a member of your family, subject to them being accepted as a potential franchisee.

Arbitration

This is designed to resolve disputes between franchisee and franchisor. This is essentially a private litigation whereby both parties appoint a judge (arbitrator) to oversee the proceedings and determine an appropriate course of action. The BFA has its own arbitration scheme available to both members and non-members which is administered by the Chartered Institute of Arbitrators. Full details of the scheme are available by contacting the BFA.

Termination

This clause covers the circumstances under which either party can terminate the agreement prior to the official date. There will often be a minimum period before you can give notice of termination. Your franchisor can terminate the agreement if you are constantly in breach of your franchise obligations and do not take the necessary steps to rectify the situation. In the event of termination you will no longer have a legal right to use your franchisor's intellectual property and for a period of time you will not be permitted to compete directly with your franchisor in another business.

ANALYSING THE FRANCHISE AGREEMENT

Your prospective franchisor will provide a copy of the franchise agreement well in advance of the date when it needs to be signed. This will give you the opportunity to analyse the document fully. Your analysis needs to be thorough in order to ensure that you fully understand every aspect of the agreement and the legal implications involved in signing it.

Understanding the meaning of the agreement

Although franchise agreements principally cover the same topics, they are not standard documents. They are individual to your particular business and their exact contents vary between franchises. They set out the restrictions and controls imposed by the franchisor for the operation of the business throughout the entire network. This is not merely for the benefit of the franchisor but also serves to protect the franchisee's rights of trading.

The agreement is provided by the franchisor and is not subject to negotiation. However, caution needs to be exercised when a franchisor is prepared to alter clauses to suit your circumstances. If there is a willingness to alter clauses to suit your case, this may also apply to others. Continuous changes to the franchise agreement may be detrimental to all franchisees.

The clauses which comprise the agreement have been incorporated for a valid reason. Any amendments made to their meaning will adversely effect the integrity of the entire document.

Seeking professional advice

It is advisable to seek independent legal advice from a solicitor with specialist franchise experience. The BFA have accredited a number of professional advisers on the basis of their skills and understanding of the franchise industry. A full list is available by contacting the BFA. In addition to the BFA, HSBC has introduced a franchise contract vetting scheme. This is operated on a fixed fee basis and utilises the experience of a specialist franchise solicitor. Further details are available by contacting any HSBC branch.

With the benefit of the professional and legal advice you have received take the opportunity to study the franchise agreement again. It is imperative that you fully understand the implications of the document and their consequences before you sign it. Do not accept clearance of the document by a solicitor if you are still unsure of the exact meaning yourself. What may constitute a perfectly normal and legally acceptable clause to a solicitor may not be acceptable to you as a condition. Do not be afraid to ask for further clarification of any clauses you are not sure about.

When the franchise agreement is signed it becomes a legally binding document. Despite the serious nature of its content, you should not view this step with trepidation. The franchise agreement is for the benefit of both parties and should be looked upon as an insurance in the event of anything going wrong. The document forms a legal basis for the working relationship between franchisor and franchisee and its aim is to establish and maintain an equal commitment by both parties for the good of the business.

RENEWING YOUR FRANCHISE AGREEMENT

The term of your initial franchise agreement will usually run for a five to seven year period. Most agreements carry an automatic right of renewal but they are subject to your continuous compliance with the franchisor's operating methods. Some franchisors may request a renewal fee or at least reserve the right to amend their service fees. The legal costs of renewing the agreement will usually be met by the franchisee, irrespective of whether or not a renewal fee is levied.

- **A renewal fee** is payable to the franchisor in exchange for the continued right to operate the franchised system.

- **A renewal charge** is made by the franchisor to cover the legal cost of renewing the franchise agreement.

Recouping your start-up costs

It is important that the length of your agreement will enable your start-up costs to be recouped. The details governing renewal will be contained within the agreement itself which needs to be very carefully scrutinised. For example, the franchisor may demand an expensive renewal fee or even reserve the right not to extend your existing agreement.

There are a number of legal implications associated with leased premises which need to be reflected within the terms of your agreement. For example, not all leases and franchise agreements run concurrently. You will need to determine who will be responsible for the lease at the end of your agreement.

Understanding revised agreements

The terms of the new agreement should be similar to the existing one or in some cases expanded upon as a result of improved working practices. There are a few unscrupulous organisations that derive a large proportion of their revenue by imposing regular renewal franchisee fees. These fees make it very difficult for franchisees to generate sufficient profits to sustain the success of their businesses.

CASE STUDIES

Joshua sells his franchise

As a gesture of goodwill and to ensure the continued success of the business, Joshua agrees to work alongside the new owner during the first few weeks. Although the new owner has been fully trained by Clean and Gleam and understands the theory behind how the franchise operates, Joshua is able to help put the theory into practice. There is a smooth managerial changeover satisfying each of the three parties: Joshua has successfully sold his business, Clean and Gleam have gained a new competent franchisee and the new owner has purchased a highly profitable company.

Jake exchanges contracts
Jake is now in a position to exchange contracts. Although the CheckElec contract is a standard document that has been used on many previous occasions, Jake decides that prior to signing and for his own peace of mind he will have it professionally examined by a solicitor. As the franchise contract is a legally binding document that sets out the legal obligations of both franchisee and franchisor, Jake wants to ensure that he fully understands what he is agreeing to. The solicitor concludes that the contract does not contain anything out of the ordinary and advises Jake to sign.

Charlotte examines the franchise fee
As her intended business is a new franchise initiative Charlotte does not have the benefit of talking to existing franchisees. However she takes the opportunity of contacting the manager of one of the shops involved in the 18-month pilot scheme. Her enquiries prove encouraging and she learns that the ongoing fees are a combined calculation of percentage turnover and mark-up on stock. The existing manager has nothing but praise for the support and help received from the franchisor. Having received confirmation from her solicitor that the document is in order, Charlotte is ready to sign her franchise agreement and start trading as soon as her new premises are available.

ACTION POINTS

1. Fully research all the facts and figures.

2. Ensure that you have the optimum location within your territorial area.

3. Make sure that the franchisor's fees are reasonable.

8

Complying with Legal Requirements

UNDERSTANDING THE TRADING FORM OF YOUR FRANCHISE

Before your franchise begins to trade you need to consider the legal form the business will take. The legal form will affect every aspect of the business, from operational issues through to the administration of major decisions. There are primarily four trading forms a business can take:

- sole trader
- partnership
- limited company
- co-operative.

As a prospective franchisee, you will probably find that co-operatives are unlikely to be an appropriate trading status. They are owned and controlled by those working within them and must represent a minimum of seven people. Therefore, from an organisational point of view, co-operatives are not easily compatible with franchised networks.

There are a variety of advantages and disadvantages associated with each business type. The type most suited to your circumstances will depend on various factors such as:

- your business requirements
- the level of financial risk
- your tax position.

Sole trader

Subject to the operating controls imposed by the franchisor, you will make all the decisions regarding how the business should be run under this arrangement. You are completely your own boss and are entitled to all the profits of the business. However, as a sole trader your business is legally regarded as one of your assets and subject to unlimited liability. This means that if your business should fail, under the terms of the Bankruptcy Acts your creditors are entitled to seize all of your personal assets. These can include your house, car, possessions and savings, but will exclude a few basic essentials necessary for yourself and your family. It is possible to avoid this scenario by transferring personal assets unconditionally to your spouse provided he or she is not a partner in the business. However, this must be done a minimum of two years prior to the onset of any financial problems and the business must be solvent.

Partnership

A **partnership** applies when between two and twenty people own the business and has the advantage of combining the financial resources and skills of all those involved in the business. In addition, responsibilities will be shared and the pressures of running a business will be reduced. Profits are shared between the partners and are taxed as income, regardless of whether or not they have been drawn.

Choosing your business partner

Partners need to be chosen with extreme care as running a business can challenge the strength of any relationship. Partnerships are essentially a group of sole traders whereby each partner is held equally liable for the business actions of the others. Therefore, your personal assets can be seized to pay for business mistakes made by other partners. Although you are not held liable for the private debts of a partner, their share of the business can be seized by creditors in the event of personal bankruptcy. This can prove financially difficult if you need to buy out their share of the business.

Limited company

A **limited company** is regarded as a separate legal entity, which means that your liability is limited to the amount of share capital you contributed. However, most lenders now stipulate that directors give personal guarantees, thus increasing the liability of the company. Unlike sole traders and partnerships, creditors are only able to make a claim against the assets of the company and not against you personally. Limited companies are the most expensive and complex type of trading status. The principal advantage of limited companies is their ability to raise capital by selling shares.

The business is controlled by a board of directors and Corporation Tax is payable on taxable profits. As a director you are regarded as a salaried employee and will be subject to National Insurance and Pay As You Earn (PAYE) tax deductions.

INFORMING THE RELEVANT AUTHORITIES

Who you need to inform and the extent of the information you need to provide is dependent on your intended trading status.

Sole traders

Sole traders are subject to the least formalities and legal considerations. You will need to register with the Inland Revenue as self-employed and will pay tax on your profits after business expenses and personal allowances have been deducted. You will be required to pay Class 2 National Insurance Contributions, and if your profits exceed certain limits Class 4 Contributions will also be due. There is no legal requirement for your accounts to be either audited or filed with Companies House.

Partnerships

Partnerships are similar to sole traders in having very few legal formalities. However, it is advisable to have a partnership agreement drawn up by a solicitor even though there is no legal requirement to do so. An agreement is used to set out details of ownership, describe each partner's obligations and resolve disputes. Where no partnership agreement exists, the Partnership Act 1890 decrees that profits and losses are to be shared equally. In the case of a limited partnership the Limited Partnership Act 1907 will also apply.

Limited companies

Limited companies are unable to start trading until a Memorandum of Association and Articles of Association have been filed with the Registrar of Companies at Companies House.

- **Memorandum of Association** is a legal document which dictates the external relationship between the company and third parties. The Memorandum must contain compulsory information regarding the name, address and financial organisation of the business.

- **Articles of Association** detail the internal relationship between the company and its shareholders. The Articles dictate the rights and duties of the shareholders in relation to how the company is administered.

Limited companies are legally required to file annual accounts with Companies House for public inspection. These accounts must be audited by a chartered or certified accountant, which can be very expensive. You can buy the name of a limited company through a registration agent or form your own using a solicitor or accountant.

VAT

Irrespective of trading status, if turnover exceeds £50,000 you will be required to register for **Value Added Tax (VAT)**. However, even if your turnover is below this figure it may still be advantageous to become VAT registered. This is particularly relevant to businesses selling zero-rated items such as food or books. Your accountant will be able to advise on your VAT position and which trading status is best suited to your needs.

If you are registered for VAT then you will be required to complete a VAT Returns Form at the end of each accounting period, normally quarterly. Following completion you will then pay, or reclaim, the outstanding amount to or from Customs and Excise.

KEEPING ACCOUNTS

Keeping detailed **financial accounts** is an important business administration task. The long-term survival of your franchise will depend on your financial information being accurate from the start. You can either keep your own accounts or use an outside agency such as an accountant or book-keeping service. It is essential that you have a financial understanding of your franchise even if you do not compile this information yourself. Independent advice from your bank and business colleagues will indicate which system is the most appropriate for your business.

Producing an accurate profit and loss account and balance sheet

There are no rules and regulations governing standard methods for keeping and preparing accountancy information. However, there are universally recognised guidelines for what financial information constitutes an adequate accounting system. Your accounts must be sufficiently detailed to produce an accurate profit and loss account and balance sheet. This information can then be used to identify, monitor and to communicate the financial position of your business to a variety of people all with different objectives. These people need to make informed judgements and decisions about your business and include:

- **yourself** – you will need to determine the profitability and financial resources of the business

- **the bank** will need to ascertain your financial position if you require any borrowing

- **potential buyers** will need to establish the value of your franchise and evaluate its previous and future development

- **potential business partners** will need to know if your franchise is profitable before deciding to buy into your business

- **investors** will need to know that your franchise represents a good investment

- **Inspector of Taxes** will use the information to calculate your tax liability.

Monitoring and maintaining your accounts
In order to be effective, business accounts need to be updated on a regular basis so that they can be used to:

- monitor and plan business performance

- prepare profit and loss accounts and balance sheets

- accurately calculate royalties and ongoing fees payable to your franchisor

- identify market trends

- help foresee any problems long before they arise

- show how much money you owe to creditors

- show how much money is owed to you by debtors

- resolve any tax dispute with the Inland Revenue

- Resolve any VAT dispute with Customs and Excise.

The method of keeping accounts best suited to your franchise will be dependent on the nature and size of your business. However, you will need to check your franchise agreement as some franchisors insist on a particular method.

Your business accounts and records need to be retained for a period of six years. An inspection of your accounts can be made at any time by the Inland Revenue and by Customs and Excise if you are VAT registered.

Generally speaking, the larger the business the more complex the accounting system will need to be. There are a variety of manual and computerised accounting systems on the market. For smaller businesses, a manual system will usually suffice. These are available from most business stationery outlets and include:

- **Simplex 'D' Accounts** – published by George Vyner Ltd
- **Essential Accounts Book** – published by Collins
- **Crown Complete Accounting** – published by Twinlock.

Larger businesses will benefit from a computerised system. The following companies have a range of software options to suit most requirements:

- **Sage** – Sage Software Ltd, Sage House, Benton Park Road, Newcastle upon Tyne NE7 7LZ. Tel: (0191) 255 3000.

- **Pegasus** – Pegasus Software Ltd, 35–41 Montagu Street, Kettering, Northants NN16 8BR. Tel: (01536) 495200.

- **Quickbooks** – Intuit Ltd, Manor Court, Harmondsworth, Middlesex UB7 0AQ. Tel: (0208) 990 5500.

It is important to choose your accounting system with care. Take independent advice and ensure your accounts will provide sufficient information regarding the financial position of your business.

INSURING YOUR FRANCHISE

All businesses are subject to unexpected events beyond their control. These events can result in financial disruption which will adversely affect the profitability of a business. The profitability of your franchise will determine your ability to:

- repay loans
- meet other financial commitments
- provide financially for any families dependent on your business.

The provision of adequate insurance policies is an important issue that needs to be properly addressed. The financial implications of being under-insured can be severe. It can even result in the failure of your franchise should you be unable to fulfil your side of the agreement.

Some areas of insurance will be your responsibility and the remainder will belong to your franchisor. These will be defined in your franchise agreement which should be read very carefully. Your franchisor will ensure you have made the necessary insurance arrangements. However, as the franchise is essentially your business, the responsibility for maintaining and renewing these policies will ultimately rest with you.

Ensuring you have adequate cover

There are some insurance areas such as employers' liability and third party motor insurance which are compulsory by law if you employ people or use vehicles for business. Other insurances such as public liability and property, are not mandatory but are highly recommended.

To be adequately insured your insurance policies need to cover both yourself and the business.

- **The protection of premises, equipment, contents and stock** – needs to cover damage as a result of fire or flood and replacement as a result of loss or theft.

- **Employers' Liability** – will provide protection against your liability in the event of accidental injury, death or disease being caused to any staff employed on your premises or place of work.

- **Public Liability** – will provide protection against legal liability in the event of accidental injury, death, or disease being caused to a member of the public either at your premises or through the course of your business.

- **Legal insurance policies** – provide prosecution protection against Acts of Parliament specific to your business, for example: unfair dismissal, fair trading and insolvency if you are a limited liability company. The Institute of Directors has developed an insurance scheme against successful claims made under the Insolvency Act. This Act was brought into effect to ensure incompetent and fraudulent directors carry a certain amount of personal liability in the event of insolvency.

- **Life insurance** – this needs to ensure that a sufficient degree of financial provision is made in the event of your death or the death of a director, key member of staff, partner or shareholder.

- **Income protection** – this can be an expensive policy but is necessary in the event of your incapacity to manage the business through either accident or illness.

EMPLOYING STAFF

Franchised business are often required to employ staff at an earlier stage than new business start-ups. This is particularly relevant in businesses difficult to operate on a one-person basis such as those in retail or fast food sectors. Employing staff is an unfamiliar area to many new franchisees yet is essential to get right if your business is to prosper. You will need to develop your interview skills or ask a business colleague to assist with the process. Recruiting the right staff is discussed further in Chapter 10, Running a Successful Franchise.

Conforming to legislation

As an employer you will need to be aware of the government's various legislative measures designed to protect the rights of your employees. This includes issues such as equal rights regardless of gender, racial origin or disability. These measures affect all employers regardless of their business size and all employees both full- and part-time. Franchised businesses are particularly affected because their operational conditions have a direct effect on the employer–employee relationship. For example, the franchise agreement will often dictate how staff are to dress or approach customers.

Calculating salaries and wages

As an employer you are legally required to deduct **PAYE** (Pay As You Earn) tax, National Insurance and other statutory contributions from your employees' pay. The Inland Revenue, Benefits Agency and the Contributions Agency have produced a New Employer's Starter Pack which contains everything you need to make these deductions accurately. This pack, together with further information, can be obtained by contacting the employers' helpline set up by the Inland Revenue, Contributions Agency and Customs and Excise on 0345 143 143. Staff here can answer general questions regarding tax, National Insurance and VAT. A flow chart detailing the PAYE and Nl process is illustrated in Figure 8.

Observing rules and regulations

This section only highlights the principal topics that need to be addressed. There are many books devoted to the legal technicalities governing the rules and regulations of employing staff. Some useful publications are listed in the Further Reading section at the end of this book.

Contract of Employment

This document should be signed by every employee working a minimum of eight hours a week within 13 weeks following the commencement of employment. The contract will define clearly the terms and conditions of employment by describing the employee's duties, hours of work, level of pay and length of holidays. In addition, the document will set out the employee's and employer's obligations to one another which can be referred to in the event of any future disagreements.

Unfair dismissal

Within two years from the start of employment you are able to give staff notice of dismissal in accordance with the terms of their contract of employment. But unfair dismissal legislation applies to staff continuously employed in the business for two years or more. Under this legislation you are unable to sack an employee without legitimate cause. Such cause can include being in breach of their contract or following a predefined number of written warnings.

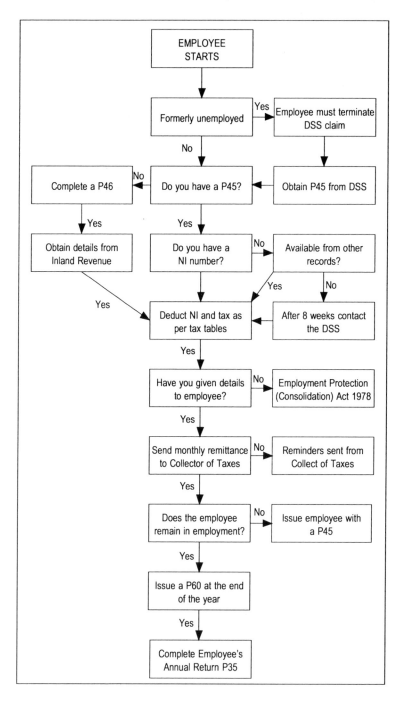

Fig. 8. A flow chart showing the PAYE and NI process.

Redundancy

As with dismissal, this only applies to staff continuously employed in the business for two years or more. The issue of **redundancy** is not extended to contractors or agency supplied personnel. Redundancy comes into effect when a particular job no longer exists. As an employer you will be legally required to meet the cost of redundancy pay. The amount of money payable to an employee will be determined by their age, length of employment and level of pay.

Health and safety

The **Health and Safety at Work Act** has been introduced to ensure business premises conform to specific standards. These standards are imposed by inspectors of the Health and Safety Executive who should be consulted prior to leasing or buying premises. In addition, the Fire Officer should also be contacted in respect of the Fire Precautions Act. The cost of altering premises to comply with this Act can be extremely expensive. Although your franchisor may undertake these checks on your behalf, the responsibility to ensure that modifications have been made, and are maintained, will rest with you.

CASE STUDIES

Joshua forms a limited company

After taking advice from his accountant Joshua decides to set up his new franchise as a limited company. This means that his liability is limited to the amount of share capital he has invested in the business. Joshua's solicitor is instructed to draw up a Memorandum of Association and Articles of Association. These documents need to be filed with the Registrar of Companies at Companies House before he can start trading. The business will be jointly owned by Joshua and his wife. Joshua's wife will take an active role in the business and she is appointed a director. She will be responsible for franchise recruitment and development. Joshua's role will be to oversee the day-to-day running of the business and to control all operational issues.

Jake must be qualified

Although Jake is a fully qualified electrician, he must undertake a specially developed CheckElec training course. The successful completion of this course is a requirement of the franchise agreement. The two-week course is run alongside his initial training programme and serves as a guarantee for the franchisor that Jake is a competent electrician. Due to the nature of the business Jake is legally required to have his own Public Liability insurance policy in the event of accident or injury. Jake passes his course which means that he is qualified to operate his business under the brand name of CheckElec.

Charlotte informs the relevant authorities

When Charlotte starts her business she will become both self-employed and an employer for the first time. She decides to contact her local tax office for advice and receives a detailed information pack. From this she learns that she has to inform the tax office officially of her change in employment status and that she will be required to make her own Class 4 National Insurance contributions. In addition she will be responsible for deducting PAYE and National Insurance contributions from her employees. Charlotte's financial projections indicate that her turnover will exceed the VAT threshold. Following advice from her accountant Charlotte decides her business should be VAT registered at the start of trading. This means that she will be able to reclaim VAT on her legitimate business expenses.

ACTION POINTS

1. Choose your trading status and if you have decided on a partnership make sure that you can work with your partner.

2. Ensure that your book-keeping and accounting systems cover all aspects of the business.

3. Make sure that your working practices and environment meet the necessary criteria for the employment of staff.

9

Becoming a Franchisee

RECEIVING YOUR INITIAL TRAINING

Arranging training dates

Your initial training programme forms an integral and important part of the franchise package. Training dates need to be arranged and agreed prior to signing the franchise agreement as this information will be contained within the document. The agreement will also include details of the duration, payment responsibilities and the number of people entitled to receive training. The cost of training is generally incorporated within the initial franchise fee. However, you will usually be expected to meet further expenses, such as travelling and possibly accommodation.

The location of your training will depend on the nature of the business. Businesses that use large or bulky equipment will obviously be limited to specific locations for their training programmes. Other training programmes will usually be held at either the franchisor's head office or an approved training facility such as a conference centre.

Confirming your training programme

Your research will have shown how long the training will last and the areas of the business that will be covered. It will be helpful to receive details of the training programme well in advance. This will give you the opportunity to ensure that the training will be sufficient for your needs. An effective training programme will have clearly defined objectives which are backed up with details of how they are to be achieved. Your training must not be restricted to the products you sell, or the service you provide, but must address all aspects of running a franchise from the operational procedures through to financial management. In addition your training will need to cover statutory obligations regarding employing staff, paying tax, national insurance and VAT.

The initial training programme will be used by your franchisor to assess your suitability as a franchisee. Franchise agreements often

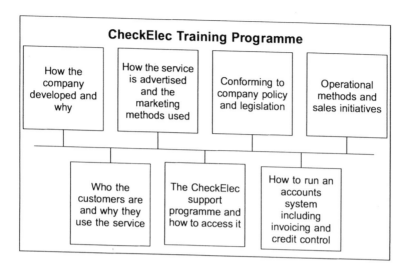

Fig. 9. A chart showing a typical training programme.

contain contingency clauses whereby the franchisor reserves the right to withdraw the opportunity prior to your agreed date of commencement. This will only occur if, during your training, the franchisor concludes that you do not have the necessary attributes to succeed.

The purpose of training is to set you up in business as soon as possible. Figure 9 shows the topics covered in an initial and ongoing training programme. You will be taught the skills and shown the methods necessary to operate your business competently. Your training should be extended to include a supervised period within your own area, although this is not always possible.

Future training requirements

Your training will involve an initial programme followed by a series of additional sessions. These sessions will be necessary as operating methods change and new products are launched. Check in advance whether this training is compulsory and who will be expected to meet the cost.

USING THE OPERATING MANUAL

The operating manual is produced by the franchisor as a comprehensive source of reference for the franchisee. The purpose of the manual is to ensure that each franchised outlet adheres to unified systems and procedures. Its contents comprise all the elements necessary to run a franchised business in accordance with the working practices of your franchisor. This will ensure that although each business is independently owned and operated the same levels of quality and customer service are consistent throughout the network.

Understanding the importance of the operating manual

The operating manual serves as a tool for the franchisor to illustrate how the business should be run on a day-to-day basis. This will enable the franchisor to maintain and retain ultimate control over the entire network.

Although the operating manual and franchise agreement are separate documents, their objectives are similar. For example, the contents of both documents:

- must be adhered to
- state precisely how the business is to be operated
- should be clearly written to ensure that no ambiguity exists for either party.

Updating the operating manual

The contents of the franchise agreement remain static throughout the term of the franchise. The operating manual, however, is a living document that is regularly amended and updated as operational methods change and develop. It is usually produced as a loose-leafed document which enables individual sections to be altered without the need to reproduce the entire manual.

Despite the importance of the manual, the document must be:

- easy to read
- easy to understand
- easy to use.

Your research will indicate when the manual was last updated and how often this is done. Operating manuals are updated on either an annual or continual basis. Continual updates are usually implemented through an official memorandum issued by the franchisor. These are later incorporated when the manual needs to be reprinted.

Changes made to the operating manual must benefit the network as a whole and not just the franchisor. Any changes that directly affect a clause within the franchise agreement must be agreed with all franchisees prior to being implemented. This is particularly relevant when these involve major expense to franchisees, such as purchasing new equipment.

Complying with the operating manual

Your franchise agreement will explain the consequences and liabilities of not adhering to the contents of the operating manual. Contravening the franchisor's operating procedures can render you in breach of your franchise agreement. In the case of a breach you will, initially, be given the opportunity to rectify the situation. Failure to do this to the satisfaction of your franchisor can result in the termination of your agreement and, ultimately the loss of your business.

SURVIVING THE FIRST MONTHS

Until now the prospect of owning your own business and becoming your own boss has been just a dream. Now that the dream has been realised, the reality of how this will affect your life will begin to set in. The first few months of any new business are often the most difficult. You will not only have to cope with learning the methods and procedures of the franchise system but you may also be self-employed for the first time. During this time it is perfectly natural to question whether you have made the right decision and if you have the ability to make a success of your business.

Adjusting to your new working environment

Even though you have fully researched your franchise and believe that you are fully committed to running your own business there will often be an initial period of second thoughts. This period of self-adjustment can be quite a shock to the system. The transition from the security of employment to being self-employed and accepting the associated risks can sometimes cause self-doubt. However, this is precisely the time when you must believe in your ability to run a successful business.

The early stages of a new business often result in expenses having to be met before sufficient sales have been generated to meet them. Although your cash flow forecast will have projected this initial lull it can be hard to cope with. At this stage your commitment is essential in order to see beyond these initial difficulties. Close reference to your business plan and future projections will enable you to monitor your progress and give you encouragement to persevere.

Consulting with your franchisor and existing franchisees

Unlike independent business start-ups, you will be able to rely on the continued help and advice from both your franchisor and existing franchisees. This support will be invaluable during the early stages of the business and will help to build your confidence. No matter how comprehensive your initial training is, there will be some situations which you are unsure how to deal with. Being able to make use of the experience of people within the franchise organisation can help overcome these problems. It is in your franchisor's interest to ensure that you succeed so never be afraid to ask for assistance.

Coping with unforeseen problems

Every business is prone to unforeseen circumstances, expenses and problems. These difficulties may be the result of a number of issues such as breakdowns or complete equipment failure. Although these can be demoralising, it is important to adopt a positive approach to such matters in order to solve these problems. Being confident in your business will enable you to do this successfully. Your confidence will grow as you set and achieve targets and will be improved further as you maintain these levels whilst aiming at new objectives.

SUCCEEDING AS A FRANCHISEE

Franchised businesses form the basis of a two-way partnership between the franchisee and the franchisor. As your confidence and familiarity with the system develops, your early reliance on the franchisor will diminish. This is when it is easy to lose sight of how franchising works and of your objectives for becoming a franchisee. It is important to remember that both parties make an equal contribution towards the combined success of the network as a whole and that one party cannot exist without the other.

Establishing a working relationship with your franchisor

You are in business with your franchisor and because of your franchisor, they are not in business because of you. Your long-term success is dependent on your ability to establish and maintain a strong working relationship with your franchisor. You must be able to work with your franchisor and not against them. It is unlikely that you will agree with all of your franchisor's working practices but your adherence to them is crucial for your business to progress.

As your business develops and you become expert in your particular field, you may begin to resent your franchisor's control and think that you know better. However, your business must be continually operated in accordance with the rules and regulations of your franchise agreement. This may prevent you from exploiting particular opportunities that you consider profitable. Alternatively, your franchisor may welcome new ideas and initiatives, provided that they can be applied to the entire network.

Monitoring your market

All franchisees aspire to a point when the business can generate a sufficient level of revenue to ensure its own profitability. Although this is a comfortable position to be in, remember that no single business ever exists in isolation, and your profitability will be influenced by market trends. You cannot afford to be complacent. Customers will come and go and you must constantly increase your client base accordingly to allow for the inevitable loss of custom whilst still maintaining your level of business.

To ensure success, you must be able to react and respond to the constant changes in market trends. Many of these changes will be recognised and nationally implemented by your franchisor. However, as a business owner you must be able to react to local trends that will not always be apparent to your franchisor. For example, the performance of the products you sell or the service you provide will vary between regions of the country. So your marketing strategy will need to reflect local buying trends which may differ from national trends.

MANAGING YOUR BUSINESS

Regardless of how simple a franchise structure appears, no business will ever run itself. Being able to manage a business is important for its long-term success.

Maintaining your motivation

During the early stages of the business your level of motivation will be extremely high because many tasks will be new. This adds to the excitement of running a business. However, as you become experienced with the franchise system your level of motivation may decline. Tasks can become mundane when they form part of a routine. Managing a business requires a continued level of motivation. You must continually challenge yourself and not lose interest in the business. One of the best ways to do this is to set yourself targets that are only just achievable. This will ensure that you are constantly striving towards goals and will help keep your level of motivation high.

Organising your workload

Know and accept your limitations. You will not have the time or the energy to complete every task personally. Delegate your workload sensibly – either to your staff or to members of your family – in order to alleviate some of the pressure and ensure that each task is completed on time.

Reviewing your situation

You must be constantly aware of how your business is doing. This can be achieved by regularly using your business plan as a tool for monitoring progress. Constant reviews will enable you to foresee any problems before they arise and, in the light of your experience, you will be able to make necessary adjustments for the future running of the business.

Managing a business does not allow for complacency and your plan will help you to adapt to your changing environment. As your business develops, so too will your long- and short-term objectives. The future development of your business will be reliant on these objectives being achieved.

CASE STUDIES

Joshua buys a new franchise

After several meetings with the American franchisor and numerous visits to the bank Joshua eventually raises the necessary finance to become a regional franchisee. Joshua's franchised area comprises twelve adjoining regions and, after a highly successful recruitment drive, all have been allocated. The sale of these areas enables Joshua to recoup a proportion of his initial investment which he reinvests in the business. It is Joshua's responsibility to oversee every aspect of the business and to ensure that the franchisees under his control conform with operational methods of the franchise.

Jake starts trading

As they do for all new franchisees, CheckElec have organised a highly successful advertising campaign through a variety of local media outlets. This, combined with the initial help and support of his area manager, enables Jake to establish his business quickly. He is determined to offer a prompt and reliable service to all his customers. Jake achieves this aim and very quickly builds a strong and regular customer base which he can develop. His enthusiasm and the high level of service he is offering soon lead to a commendable reputation purely by recommendation. His workload grows rapidly and he very quickly has to plan his days carefully to maintain his commitment to newly established customers and yet still cater for new business.

Charlotte opens for business

Following a highly intensive training course, Charlotte finally opens the doors of her Movie Store franchise. The franchisor has found Charlotte a prime location within a newly built shopping complex near a large multiplex. Although the responsibilities of a business owner are considerably greater than those of a business manager, Charlotte has adapted well to the change. She initially employs two members of staff – which quickly increases to three – to assist with the day-to-day running of the business. Being new to franchising, the Movie Store want to ensure that Charlotte's business will succeed and accordingly they give her all the help and advice they possibly can.

ACTION POINTS

1. Arrange and confirm your training dates prior to signing the franchise agreement.

2. Consult your franchisor and existing franchisees for help, advice and moral support.

3. Maintain your motivation by constantly monitoring and renewing your targets.

10

Running a Successful Franchise

DEVELOPING YOUR BUSINESS

As well as being a legal obligation under the terms and conditions of your franchise agreement, developing your business is of paramount importance if your franchise is to succeed. No market ever remains static and all businesses are subject to the effects of changes in market trends. You must be able to react positively to the needs of your changing environment and the pressures of the competition. Your business must be adaptable so that it can continue to meet the requirements of your continuously changing customer base.

Remaining competitive

Both you and the franchisor will need to be constantly aware of the competition and understand how this will affect the development of your business. Then you will be able to establish areas for improvement and stay ahead of the competition. Possible opportunities may be identified that cannot be fully exploited as they fall outside the current parameters of the franchise agreement. However, most franchisors welcome suggestions for improvements, provided they can be seen to benefit the entire network. Some franchisors even reward their franchisees with financial incentives for making suggestions that can be successfully implemented.

Implementing changes

Revised methods are designed to improve and benefit the network as a whole and they need to be jointly implemented by both parties. These improvements may involve additional investment if equipment needs to be updated or replaced. This can often cause conflict between you and the franchisor, particularly if you are unable to finance these costs. However, your franchisor must remain within the boundaries of the franchise agreement. Any improvements, or modifications, that affect the clauses contained within the agreement must be sanctioned by all franchisees before being implemented.

Forecasting your future direction

The direction your business will take will depend on your ability to forecast the next phase of its development. This can only be achieved by monitoring every aspect of the business and implementing any necessary changes – whether to staff levels, equipment or stock as your business reacts to both seasonal and general business trends.

There are many ways to develop your business but it is generally much more cost effective to improve your existing products or services for your current customers rather than establish new markets. Your terms of trading as detailed in your franchise agreement may prevent you from directly exploiting such opportunities as an individual. Your planning needs to incorporate areas of improvement that are feasible within the remit of your agreement.

MAXIMISING YOUR BUSINESS POTENTIAL

Once your franchise becomes established it is easy to become so preoccupied with the day-to-day running that the potential it presents is neglected. As your business becomes profitable it is all too easy to become complacent. This should be avoided at all costs to prevent the road to success very quickly becoming the road to failure.

Planning your long-term objectives

As with any business, making a profit is obviously a major consideration. However, this should not be your sole aim and the potential of your franchise should be geared towards achieving your long-term business objectives. These may involve retiring at a certain age or generating financial security. Whatever your intentions are, it is important that your business remains profitable during the whole time it is in operation and not just on the point of resale. Profits can be used for a multitude of purposes including reinvestment to fund the growth of the business. Alternatively, you may wish to relinquish control by employing a manager, which in turn will give you more time to pursue other activities.

Improving performance

In order to get as much out of the business as possible you need to realise its full potential. This can be achieved by comparing actual performance against your future sales forecasts and making any necessary adjustments. For example, you may need to alter your pricing structure in order to increase sales. However, you will need

The Movie Store Cash flow Forecast – Year 2

MONTH	1	2	3	4	5	6	7	8	9	10	11	12	Total
Receipts													
Sales	5000	6000	7000	7000	7000	7500	7500	7500	8000	8000	8500	8500	87500
Capital introduced	0	0	2000	0	0	0	0	0	0	0	0	0	2000
Loans	0	0	0	0	0	0	0	0	0	0	0	0	0
Total receipts	5000	6000	9000	7000	7000	7500	7500	7500	8000	8000	8500	8500	89500
Payments													
Stock	500	750	750	750	750	750	800	800	800	800	800	800	9050
Salaries/Wages	750	750	1100	1100	1100	1100	1100	1100	1100	1100	1100	1100	12500
Rent	500	500	500	500	500	500	500	500	500	500	500	500	6000
Water Rates	150	0	0	150	0	0	150	0	0	150	0	0	600
Electricity & Gas	150	0	0	150	0	0	150	0	0	150	0	0	600
Postage	50	50	50	50	50	50	50	50	50	50	50	50	600
Business Stationery	125	125	125	125	125	125	125	125	125	125	125	125	1500
Insurance (Business)	0	0	0	0	400	400	0	0	0	0	0	0	400
Advertising	200	200	300	200	200	200	200	200	150	150	150	150	2300
Telephone	0	0	450	0	0	500	0	0	500	0	0	500	1950
Sundries	75	75	75	75	75	100	100	100	100	100	100	100	1075
Capital Items	0	0	200	0	500	0	0	0	500	0	0	0	1200
Professional Charges	0	0	0	0	0	0	0	750	0	0	0	0	750
Customs & Excise (VAT)	0	0	2000	0	0	2500	0	0	2750	0	0	3000	10250
Bank & Interest Charges	55	55	55	65	65	65	65	65	65	65	70	70	760
Other	0	0	45	0	0	45	0	0	45	0	0	45	180
Total payments	2555	2505	5650	3165	3365	6335	3240	3690	6685	3190	2895	6440	49715
Net Cash flow	2445	3495	3350	3835	3635	1165	4260	3810	1315	4810	5605	2060	39785
Opening bank balance b/f	2500	4945	8440	11790	15625	19260	20425	24685	28495	29810	34620	40225	0
Closing bank balance c/f	4945	8440	11790	15625	19260	24685	24685	28495	29810	34620	40225	42285	39785

Fig. 10. A sample cash flow forecast.

to consider how this will affect your profit margin. A price increase can result in lower sales volumes which may reduce a profit margin instead of improving it. Your business plan can be utilised for this purpose. This performance comparison will ensure that you have adequate resources to meet demand.

Utilising your cash flow forecasts
Your cash flow forecast is very similar to the profit and loss, containing many of the same headings, but it should show the expected rise and fall of your bank balance. This can be used to calculate when additional finance may be required. Figure 10 shows a sample cash flow forecast.

Making provision for plant and machinery
Your franchise needs to be planned according to the length of time you intend to keep it. Plant and equipment is often leased over a number of years, which can cause financial and legal problems if you intend to sell the business prior to the expiry of a lease.

If the business is reliant on expensive equipment, provision needs to be made for maintenance and replacement, as necessary. A business may be currently profitable but if large financial investment is necessary for updating and improving machinery it will be reflected in the value for resale.

RECRUITING THE RIGHT STAFF

All successful businesses need to recruit staff at some point. Staff are one of the most important assets that you will buy as they can directly affect the success of your franchise. So it is important to recruit the right person for the right job. In fact, your franchise agreement may stipulate that you only recruit people with relevant previous experience. This usually occurs in technical franchises, such as service engineers or car mechanics, where an employee's standard of work can affect the integrity of the entire network.

Compiling a job description
The first stage is to decide what job you want done and then compile a list of tasks that comprise that job. This list will form the basis of a job description and will highlight any qualifications that are needed. The more you know about what the job will involve, the greater chance you have of finding the most suitable candidate.

Finding the right staff

Advertising at your local employment centre or in a newspaper will generate the greatest interest. Your advertisement must be as specific as possible and must define the job and its responsibilities. All prospective applicants should be asked to complete a hand-written application form. This will indicate their ability to cope with simple paperwork and will also eliminate unsuitable applicants at the outset.

Although done with the best of intentions, recruiting family and friends to paid positions should be avoided at all costs. You must always be in a position to discipline or dismiss staff without embarrassment or consequent repercussions. Having to reprimand or sack a friend, or a family member, can cause all kinds of problems.

Interviewing prospective employees

The nature of the job will determine the best methods of recruitment. For example, the suitability of an assistant manager cannot be gauged from a short interview and an application form. You will need to take up references and conduct further interviews. In contrast, a general assistant can be selected from an initial interview but it is still important to take up references. Before inviting a prospective candidate for interview be clear on the information you require from them and what you want to know about them. Compile a comprehensive list of questions to cover all aspects relevant to the position you are offering. Combining an application form, an interview and references should enable you to find a competent, reliable and trustworthy member of staff.

Appointing staff

You are required by law to issue all employees with a contract of employment within 13 weeks of starting work. This document is for the benefit of both parties and should include details of:

- job title and description of work
- commencement date of employment
- details of remuneration and payment details
- normal hours of work and their terms and conditions
- holiday entitlement and holiday pay
- details of sick pay and arrangements
- pension details if applicable
- period of notice or length of employment

- rules regarding disciplinary procedures
- grievance procedures.

Looking after your staff

Appointing a member of staff is not the end of the recruitment process but merely the beginning. Too many employers simply leave employees to get on with their jobs with little regard to monitoring their progress. Regular employment reviews and continued staff training will ensure that your employees retain their motivation and gain job satisfaction. The Further Reading section at the end of this book contains a list of helpful publications in this area.

MAINTAINING YOUR OPTIMUM PROFITABILITY

Whatever franchise you operate some elements of the business will be more profitable than others. In order to achieve and maintain optimum profitability you will need to review the growth of your franchise constantly. This will ensure that your resources can be concentrated on developing areas with higher profit margins.

Knowing your break-even point

To determine which areas are more profitable than others you will need to monitor closely your break-even point. This is the point at which sales are exactly equal to the cost of achieving them. Your break-even point can be calculated by applying the following formula:

$$\text{Break-even} = \frac{\text{Overheads}}{\text{Gross profit margin \%}} \times 100$$

As you can see, your break-even point is not only dependent on your gross profit (the difference between your selling price and the direct cost of achieving it), but also on your total overheads.

It is quite feasible that your gross profit margin may vary from month to month. Figure 11 shows how to calculate break-even point. The example shows the calculations based on the figures for a full quarterly period but if the same equations were applied to the monthly figures the results would be very different. The most appropriate period for your business will be determined by its nature and how susceptible it is to seasonal/market changes.

Fine Finishings (*Interior Design & Fittings Specialists*)
Profit and Loss – January–March 20XX

	January		February		March		Total
Sales		40,000		12,000		28,000	80,000
Less cost of goods sold							
Materials	26,250		4,520		11,500		42,270
Carriage & packing	1,500	27,750	800	5,320	700	12,200	3,000 / 45,270
Gross Profit		**12,250**		**6,680**		**15,800**	**34,730**
Overheads							
Wages (inc. drawings)	3,900		4,400		4,600		12,900
Rent	800		800		800		2,400
Rates	325		325		325		975
Electricity	0		0		375		375
Water	0		120		0		120
Insurance	135		135		690		960
Stationery & postage	16		10		165		191
Telephone	340		41		52		433
Motor expenses	600		250		635		1,485
Other expenses	48		53		760		861
Finance costs	220	6,384	150	6,284	200	8,602	570 / 21,270
Net Profit		**5,866**		**396**		**7,198**	**13,460**

The following calculations are based on the total quarterly figures for January–March 20XX:

Calculate gross profit margin:

$$\frac{\text{Gross profit £34,730} \times 100}{\text{Sales £80,000}} = \text{gross profit margin 43.41\%}$$

Calculate actual turnover needed to break even:

$$\frac{\text{Overheads £21,270} \times 100}{\text{Gross profit margin 43.41}} = \text{break-even sales £48,998}$$

Calculate monthly turnover needed to break even:

$$\frac{\text{Break-even sales £48,998}}{\text{(3 months)}} = \text{monthly break-even sales £16,333}$$

Fig. 11. A sample profit and loss used to calculate break-even point.

Making sure your time is cost effective

You will also need to monitor and review your general business administration to ensure that all resources are being utilised in the most cost-effective way. You, and your staff, need to make the best use of your time. It is far better to pay a qualified book-keeper for one hour than to spend five hours yourself struggling with accounts. Your expertise can then be fully used in a more profitable way.

Using computer systems

Computers have become a vital component for most businesses but they are rarely maximised to their full potential. Most franchisors have developed their own computerised systems. These programs are generally designed to streamline a network and they often neglect to incorporate management tasks. Many commercial programs can be run alongside your franchisor's software that will help maintain your profitability. With so many programs it can be difficult to choose the right package for your franchise. However, by taking the right advice you can maintain your profitability by using a computer to complete tasks both more quickly and more cost effectively. For example, even a simple database can be used to highlight sales patterns, monitor customer spending and send sales letters.

Assessing future sales patterns

Computer generated information can be used to evaluate profitability by conducting a hypothetical analysis of alternatives. By using your sales forecasts and actual sales figures you can explore your various options for improvements. These hypothetical comparisons will eliminate non-productive ideas and highlight viable possibilities without involving you in major expense.

Depending on the nature of your business your sales may vary greatly from month to month, especially if you are involved in lengthy projects. Figure 11 shows how to calculate your break-even point and by analysing the sales figures in terms of type of job for that period you can find your most profitable area of work. This information can be used in projecting your future sales and highlighting the areas for improvement.

SEEKING PROFESSIONAL GUIDANCE

Throughout this book you have been encouraged to seek further advice, usually in areas of the business that require expertise beyond the scope of this book, or any book, to provide. You will not be able to leave tasks that you do not understand to others to resolve. As a business owner, the responsibility to discover and apply the relevant information will rest with you.

But it must be the right advice. Poor or misleading advice can prove detrimental to the success of your business. However, first you need to determine exactly what help you are looking for – general business advice or specialist professional advice.

General business advice

General business advice can be obtained by contacting the following organisations:

- British Franchise Association (BFA)
- Business Link
- Chamber of Commerce
- Federation of Small Businesses.

British Franchise Association (BFA)

The BFA is covered in more detail in Chapter 3, Gathering Information. The BFA is a self-regulatory body which has been established to monitor and control businesses which operate within the franchise sector. The Association can provide a tremendous amount of franchising information and should be the first organisation you contact.

Business Link

This is a national network of independent business centres. It offers advice, information and professional services on a wide range of topics from generating new business to increasing your profits. Details of your nearest Business Link can be obtained from your local telephone directory or by calling 0345 567 765. Alternatively, you can either write to Business Link, Freepost Lon13319, London EC4B 4HF or visit www.businesslink.co.uk on the internet.

Chamber of Commerce

This is an organisation which provides a forum for local businesses to discuss matters of mutual interest. In addition, the Chamber provides a range of services including information on local, national and international business opportunities. Details of your nearest Chamber of Commerce can be obtained from your local telephone directory or by contacting Business Link.

Federation of Small Businesses
This is a non-profit making organisation supported solely by members' subscriptions and donations. It operates on both local and national levels as a non-party-political lobbying group continually campaigning government bodies to improve the rights of business owners. In addition, it provides a range of membership services, including a free legal and insurance package and a number of money saving offers. The Federation can be contacted at 32 Orchard Road, Lytham St Annes, Lancashire FY8 1 NY, Tel: (01253) 720911, or on the internet at http://www.fsb.org.uk.

Specialist professional advice
After contacting the above organisations you will have a greater understanding of exactly what advice you need. Professional advisers are generally only proficient in a specific aspect of the business. Therefore you will probably need to contact a combination of advisers before you have all the information you need. Professional specialised business advisers include:

- accountants
- solicitors
- insurance brokers
- trade associations.

Accountants
Accountants can be used for a variety of reasons ranging from evaluating the finances of an established business to giving advice on the franchisor's projected figures. You need to have total confidence in your accountant and word of mouth recommendations from a source that you trust may be the best way of finding one. As a new business you will need reliable accountancy advice so ensure that your accountant is fully experienced and well established. Details of BFA accredited accountants are available by contacting the BFA.

Solicitors
The same methods for finding an accountant should be applied to finding a solicitor. All solicitors are experienced in a particular aspect of law so ensure that your solicitor specialises in commercial business matters and, if possible, franchising. Details of BFA accredited solicitors are available by contacting the BFA.

Insurance brokers
These are not bound to a particular insurance company. Insurance is a highly competitive market and an experienced broker will be able to shop around on your behalf to secure the best deal. Insurance is an important aspect of the business but is often overlooked as being unnecessary and too expensive. You will need to consider liability insurance to cover business risks and general insurance to cover property, equipment and staff.

Trade associations
These will be able to provide a variety of information which is specific to your industry. This can be very useful during the early stages of your business research, especially when analysing the potential of the franchise opportunity. Statistical information is particularly useful, especially when it is applied and utilised within your business plan. Your local Chamber of Commerce will be able to provide you with the address of your local trade association.

CASE STUDIES

Joshua's first trading year is a success
At the end of his first trading year Joshua has exceeded his initial financial projections and has generated a surplus of revenue. Joshua decides to keep his money invested in the business and increases his marketing and advertising expenditure. This proves to be a worthwhile investment as both turnover and profitability rise, leading to an increased level of business and the introduction of a further three franchisees. Joshua is now in a position to appoint a general manager to both alleviate some of the pressure and enable him to spend time with his family. Joshua's success has been achieved as a direct result of combining hard work with an overwhelming desire to succeed.

Jake monitors his progress
The first few months are very busy and consequently Jake falls behind with his invoicing. Despite the fact that he needs to spend all his time working Jake is aware that his accounting is as important as the practical side of his business. If he does not keep up to date with his paperwork then he will quickly encounter cash flow problems and will be unable to pay his own bills. This inefficiency could ultimately lead to the end of his business despite the fact that his

work and reputation are first class. Jake decides to employ a part-time administration clerk to deal with invoicing and general correspondence. This allows Jake to concentrate on expanding his client base and increasing his turnover.

Charlotte's business is a success
At the end of her first trading year Charlotte has managed to surpass all of her projections. This is encouraging news for both Charlotte's bank manager and her franchisor who can now refer to her success when speaking to prospective franchisees. Charlotte's success has been achieved by combining the support of her franchisor with her own hard work and determination to succeed. By the end of the second year Charlotte's store has become so busy that she has relocated the business to new premises, which has enabled her to increase her range of merchandise and generate more sales.

ACTION POINTS

1. Define your long-term objectives for your business.

2. Compile job descriptions and an interview checklist for prospective employees.

3. Contact business organisations and enlist professional support services where necessary.

Glossary

Articles of Association. These detail the internal relationship between the company and its shareholders. The Articles dictate the rights and duties of the shareholders in relation to how the company is administered.

Associate BFA franchisors. These are companies who have financed and managed a successful pilot scheme for at least 12 months. In addition they must be able to provide evidence of successful franchising over a one-year period with at least one franchisee.

British Franchise Association (BFA). This is the self-regulating body for franchising throughout the United Kingdom.

Business plan. This is used both to present your proposal to prospective lenders and by those who will be responsible for managing the business and planning on a day-to-day basis.

Capital repayment holiday. This facility is sometimes offered by the lender for a predetermined period, usually between six and eighteen months, and is designed to ease cash flow during the early stages of the business. It is particularly useful for businesses which will not initially generate surplus revenue but will be able to meet larger repayments at a later date.

Confidentiality agreement. This is a short simple document under which the prospective franchisee agrees not to disclose or use any information concerning the operating methods or practices of the franchisor.

Contract of employment. This document defines the terms and conditions of employment by describing the employee's duties, hours of work, level of pay and length of holidays.

Contract hire. This is very similar to an operating lease but usually includes additional services, such as maintenance and servicing.

Employer's liability insurance. This provides protection against liability in the event of accidental injury, death or disease being caused to staff.

Executive franchises. These provide services for business executives in areas such as accountancy, cost reduction, project management and consultancy.

Factoring. A service provided by a factoring company which 'buys' a franchisee's unpaid invoices, enabling them to receive 80 per cent of the money due to them straightaway. The rest is payable when the remaining balance is recovered, less the factoring company's handling charge.

Finance lease. The legal ownership of the asset is retained by the franchise company until the asset is sold at the end of the lease period.

Franchise agreement. This document acts as a safeguard to protect the rights of each party, franchisor and franchisee, by setting out their legal obligations towards one another.

Franchise loans. These are specially designed by banks to finance the cost of the franchise or to develop the business at a later date.

Franchise prospectus. This is a descriptive brochure provided by the franchisor as an overview to their particular franchise.

Franchising. A business owner (a franchisor) sells the licensed rights to duplicate the business to a business operator (a franchisee) in exchange for a continuing service fee.

Full BFA franchisors. These companies have financed and managed a successful pilot scheme for at least 12 months. In addition they must provide evidence of successful franchising over a two-year period with a minimum of four franchisees.

Hire Purchase. Buying an asset on credit terms which, after making the final payment, enables you to own the asset. For tax purposes the asset is regarded as yours from the beginning.

Income protection. This can be an expensive policy but is necessary in the event of an incapacity to manage the business through either accident or illness.

Initial fees. These are one-off fees payable to the franchisor to cover the cost of setting up a new franchise.

Intellectual property. This is what the franchisor owns in terms of copyright material, trade marks, trade names, and operating methods.

Investment franchise. This involves a substantial capital investment into a franchise concept such as a major hotel or restaurant chain.

Job franchise. A franchisee purchases the right to operate a one-person business. This type of franchise usually requires a lower level of financial investment and is often dependent on specialist qualifications such as an electrician or motor engineer.

Lease purchase. From the perspective of tax the asset is treated in the same manner as hire purchase. However, ownership is deferred until the end of the agreement when a final lump sum payment is made.

Life insurance. This needs to ensure that a sufficient degree of financial provision is made in the event of the death, particularly of a director or a key member of staff, partner or shareholder.

Limited company. Is regarded as a separate legal entity which means that financial liability is limited to the amount of capital contributed.

Management franchise. The franchise coordinates a group of operatives throughout several territories or within a defined region.

Management service fees. These are regularly paid to the franchisor in return for the management services provided by the franchisor such as advice, training and support.

Memorandum of Association. This is a legal document which dictates the external relationship between the company and all third parties.

Ongoing fees. These are payable to the franchisor in respect of continued services provided by the franchisor.

Operating lease. This is similar to a finance lease except that the asset is returned to the finance company at the end of the lease period.

Operating manual. This document dictates the operational procedures of each franchisor to which every franchisee must conform.

Overdraft. This is the most popular and cost-effective method of borrowing for short-term financial needs such as working capital.

Partnerships. These apply when between two and twenty people own a business. A partnership combines the financial resources and skills of all those involved in the business, and profits and responsibilities are shared.

Provisional BFA franchisors. These are companies in the process of developing the structure of their opportunity in association with accredited professional advice.

Public liability insurance. This provides protection against legal liability in the event of accidental injury, death or disease being caused to a member of the public either at their premises or through the course of the business.

Purchase agreement. This short document (sometimes called an option agreement) sets out the conditions of purchase between both parties and is used by the franchisor to sell a franchised territory and the purchaser to secure one.

Renewal charge. This is made by the franchisor to cover the legal cost of renewing the franchise agreement.

Renewal fee. This is payable to the franchisor in exchange for the continued right to operate the franchise system.

Retail franchises. These require a large financial investment in business premises, fittings, equipment and employees in order to operate a high turnover business system.

Royalty fees. Fees payable by the franchisee for the legal right to use the franchisor's brand name.

Sales and distribution franchises. These involve the franchisee selling and distributing products direct to the clients.

Small Firms Loan Guarantee Scheme (LGS). This government-backed scheme enables small independent businesses to obtain finance which would have otherwise been unavailable due to their lack of loan security.

Sole traders. Although subject to the operating controls imposed by the franchisor, sole traders are self-employed, able to make their own decisions regarding how the business should be run, and entitled to all profits of the business. The business is regarded as an asset and subject to unlimited liability.

Start-up costs. These vary between franchises but incorporate every expense involved with setting up a business such as premises, equipment and stock.

Working capital. This term describes the money required to finance the day-to-day running of the business.

Value Added Tax (VAT). This is a charge levied by HM Customs and Excise as a percentage of turnover on all sales over a predetermined threshold. The outstanding amount is paid or claimed on a regular basis.

Useful Addresses

BANKERS

Barclays Bank plc, Franchise Department, PO Box 120, Longwood Close, Westwood Business Park, Coventry CV4 8JN. Tel: (02476) 534433.

HSBC, Franchise Unit, 10 Lower Thames Street, London EC3R 6AE. Tel: (0207) 260 6783.

Lloyds TSB Bank plc, Retail Banking UKRB, PO Box 112 Canon's Way, Bristol BS99 7LB. Tel: (0117) 943 3410.

National Westminster Bank plc, Retail Banking Services, Franchise Section, Level 10 Drapers Gardens, 12 Throgmorton Avenue, London EC2N 2DL. Tel: (0207) 920 5966.

The Royal Bank of Scotland plc, Franchise and Licensing Department, PO Box 31, 42 St Andrew's Square, Edinburgh EH2 2YE. Tel: (0131) 523 2178.

CHARTERED ACCOUNTANTS

Fraser Russell, Albany House, 128 Station Road, Redhill, Surrey RH1 1ET. Tel: (01737) 765451.

Kidsons Impey, Carlton House, 31–34 Railway Street, Chelmsford, Essex CM1 1NJ. Tel: (01245) 269595.

Levy Gee, 66 Wigmore Street, London W1H 0HQ. Tel: (0207) 467 4000.

Pannel Kerr Forster, 78 Carlton Place, Glasgow G5 9TH. Tel: (0141) 429 5900.

Rees Pollock, 7 Pilgrim Street, London EC4V 6DR. Tel: (0207) 329 6404.

EXHIBITION ORGANISERS

Blenheim Events, Miller Freeman, Blenheim House, 630 Chiswick High Road, London W4 5BG. Tel: (0208) 742 2828.

CDFEX, 78 Carlton Place, Glasgow G5 9TH. Tel: (0141) 429 5900.
CII, 105 Lancaster Road, London W11 1QF. Tel: (0207) 727 7380.

FRANCHISE CONSULTANTS

Baker Tiley, 2 Bloomsbury Street, London WC1B 3ST. Tel: (0207) 413 5100.

BDO Stoy Hayward Management Consultants, 8 Baker Street, London W1M 1DA. Tel: (0207) 486 5888.

Dewar-Healing Associates, 20 Blythswood Square, Glasgow G2 4AR. Tel: (0141) 211 4600.

Format F, New Garden House, 78 Hatton Garden, London EC1N 8JA. Tel: (0207) 831 7393.

The Franchise Company, 70 Brunswick Street, Stockton, Cleveland TS18 1DW. Tel: (01642) 603434.

Franchise Development Services Ltd, Castle House, Castle Meadow, Norwich NR2 1PJ. Tel: (01603) 620301.

Franchise & Marketing Management Limited (FMM), 46–48 Thornhill Road, Streetly, Sutton Coldfield, West Midlands B74 3EH. Tel: (0121) 353 0031.

The Franchise Training & Consultancy Centre, 212 Piccadilly, London W1V 9LD. Tel: (0207) 917 2837.

FRANCHISE LAWYERS

Beveridge, Ross Prevezer, 10–11 New Street, London EC2M 4TP. Tel: (0207) 626 1533.

Eversheds, Senator House, 85 Queen Victoria Street, London EC4V 4JL. Tel: (0207) 919 4500.

Parker Bullen Solicitors, 45 Castle Street, Salisbury, Wiltshire SP1 3SS. Tel: (01722) 412000.

Wragge & Co, 55 Colmore row, Birmingham B2 5JY. Tel: (0121) 233 1000.

INSURANCE BROKERS

Tolsen Messenger Ltd, 148 King Street, London W6 0QU. Tel: (0208) 741 8361.

Wilde & Co, PO Box 112, Pollet House, Lower Pollet, St Peter Port, Guernsey GY1 4EA. Tel: (01481) 726446.

MEDIA AND COMMUNICATIONS

Business Franchise Magazine, Blenheim House, 630 Chiswick High
Road, London W4 5BG. Tel: (01925) 724326.

The Express 'Business Plus', Ludgate House, 245 Blackfrairs Road,
London SE1 9UX. Tel: (0207) 928 8000. The official newspaper to
the British Franchise Association.

The Franchise Magazine, Castle House, Castle Meadow, Norwich
NR2 1PJ. Tel: (01603) 620301.

Franchise World, James House, 37 Nottingham Road, London
SW17 7EA. Tel: (0208) 7671371.

Further Reading

ANNUAL TRADE DIRECTORIES

Business Franchise Directory, a definitive guide to choosing, buying and setting up a successful franchise. Available from Tower Publishing Services, Sovereign Park, Market Harborough, Leicester LE16 9EF.

Franchise World Directory, a complete breakdown of UK franchises including setting-up costs, fees, sales and profit levels. Available from *Franchise World*, James House, 37 Nottingham Road, London SW17 7EA. Tel: (0208) 767 1371.

The United Kingdom Franchise Directory, provides invaluable advice on current franchise opportunities laid out in an easy-to-compare format. Available from *The Franchise Magazine*, Castle House, Castle Meadow, Norwich NR2 1PJ. Tel: (01603) 620301.

BUSINESS MATTERS

Better Business Intelligence, Bob Collins (Management Books 2000, 1998).

Create That Change, Steve Smith (Kogan Page, 1998).

Getting More Business, Sallyann Sheridan (How To Books, 1999).

Great Myths of Business, William Davis (Kogan Page, 1998).

The Growing Business Handbook, Richard Willshaw and Adrian Jolly (Kogan Page, 1998).

How to Prepare a Marketing Plan, John Stapleton and Michael Thomas (Gower, 1998).

How to Work From Home, Ian Phillipson (How To Books, 2nd edition 1995).

Learning New Job Skills, Laurel Alexander (How To Books, 1997).

Making Decisions, Dean Juniper (How To Books, 1998).

Managing Meetings, Ann Dobson (How To Books, 1996).

Managing Your Time, Julie-Ann Amos (How To Books, 1998).

Preparing A Wining Business Plan, Matthew Record (How To Books, 3rd edition 2000).

Principles of Small Business, Colin Barrow and Robert Brown (International Thomson Publishing, 1998).

Self-Management and Personal Effectiveness, Julie-Ann Amos (How To Books, 2nd edition, 1999).

Starting to Manage, Julie-Ann Amos (How To Books, 1996).

BUSINESS SKILLS

30 Minutes to Make the Right Impression, Eleri Sampson (Kogan Page, 1998).

30 Minutes to Master the Internet, Neil Barrett (Kogan Page, 1997).

30 Minutes to Negotiate a Better Deal, Brian Finch (Kogan Page, 1998)

101 Ways to Boost Customer Satisfaction, Timothy R. V. Foster (Kogan Page, 1998).

Conducting Effective Negotiations, Patrick Forsyth (How To Books, 1997).

Managing Performance, Jenny Hill (Gower, 1998).

The Sage Guide To Setting Up and Managing Your Own Business Colin Barrow (Kensington West Productions, 1998).

DEALING WITH PEOPLE

30 Minutes to Deal With Difficult People, Cary Cooper and Valerie Sutherland (Kogan Page, 1998).

Delivering Customer Service, Sheila Payne (How To Books, 2nd edition 1999).

How To Employ And Manage Staff, Wendy Wyatt (How To Books, 1995).

Investing In People, Harley Turnbull (How To Books, 1996).

Managing Individual Performance, Kieran Baldwin (How To Books, 1999).

Managing Performance Reviews, Nigel Hunt (How To Books, 4th edition 1999).

Managing Successful Teams, John Humphries (How To Books, 1998).

Managing Through People, John Humphries (How To Books, 3rd edition 1998).

Managing Your Sales Team, John Humphries (How To Books, 2nd edition, 1999).
New Employee Induction, Charles M. Caldwell (Kogan Page, 1998).
Organising Effective Training, James Chalmers (How To Books, 1996).
Recruiting for Results, Steven Kneeland (How To Books, 1999).
Taking On Staff, David Greenwood (How To Books, 1996).
Train and Develop Your Staff, Alan George (Gower, 1998).

FINANCIAL MATTERS

The Accounting Jungle, Bill Jamieson (Management Books 2000, 1998).
A Borrower's Guide To Banks, Bankers and Bankruptcy, Keith McIlory (Management Books 2000, 1998).
Cash Flows and Budgeting Made Easy, Peter Taylor (How To Books, 3rd edition 2000).
Financial Planning Using Spreadsheets, Sue Nugus (Kogan Page, 1998).
Implementing Successful Credit Control, Alan Dixie (Management Books 2000, 1998).
Managing Credit, Roy Hedges (How To Books, 1997).
Managing Your Business Accounts, Peter Taylor (How To Books, 5th edition 1999).
Mastering Book-Keeping, Peter Marshall (How To Books, 4th edition 1999).

FRANCHISE PERIODICALS

The British Franchise Association Annual Survey of Franchising, this in-depth survey is sponsored by the Nat West and is available from the BFA.
Business Franchise, 'The Official British Franchise Association journal' is published 10 times a year and is available at large newsagents and on subscription from 630 Chiswick High Road, London W4 5BG. Tel: (01925) 724326.
Franchise International, published quarterly and available at large newsagents or by subscription from Castle House, Castle Meadow, Norwich NR2 1PJ. Tel: (01603) 620301.
The Franchise Magazine, published bi-monthly and available at large newsagents or on subscription from Castle House, Castle

Meadow, Norwich NR2 1PJ. Tel: (01603) 620301.

Franchise World, published bi-monthly and available by subscription from James House, 37 Nottingham Road, London SW17 7EA. Tel: (0208) 767 1371.

FRANCHISING

Buying Your First Franchise, Greg Clarke (Kogan Page, 2nd edition 1997).

The Ethics of Franchising (BFA, 1981).

The Franchise Option: A Legal Guide, Mark Abell (BFA 1987).

The Guide to Franchising, Martin Mendelsohn (Cassell, 5th edition 1995).

How to Evaluate a Franchise, Martin Mendelsohn (BFA, 1997).

How to Franchise Your Business, Martin Mendelsohn and David Acheson (BFA, 1982).

LEGAL MATTERS

Setting Up a Limited Company, Robert Browning (How To Books, 2nd edition 1999).

Index

accounts, 87
advertising, 58
advisory literature, 35
arbitration, 80
Articles of Association, 87
assessing
  the franchise, 67, 69, 73
  the franchisor, 46
Associate BFA membership, 31

balance sheet, 87
BFA, 31, 33, 112
break-even point, 109–110
business format franchise, 11
Business Link, 112
business plan, 53–55

capital repayment holiday, 61
cash flow forecasts, 55, 106,
  107
Chamber of Commerce, 112
checklist for prospective
  franchisee, 38–39
competition, 49, 54, 63
compiling research, 41
computer systems, 111
conditions of purchase, 75
confidentiality agreement, 73
continuing costs, 18
contract of employment, 92
contract hire, 58
criteria of BFA membership,
  32
Customs and Excise, 87

death of franchisee, 80
demand for product/service, 63
deposit, 72

employer's liability insurance,
  90
employing staff, 91, 107–109
evaluating a franchise, 12, 67
executive franchise, 12
exhibitions, 44
existing franchisees, 68

factoring, 62
Federation of Small Business,
  113
finance
  lease, 57
  schemes, 60
  sources of, 60
financial status, 25, 27
fixed assets, 57
franchise
  agreement, 78, 80
  fee, 71
  loans, 61
franchisee recruitment, 67
franchising
  advantages of, 16, 48
  definition, 11, 12
  disadvantages of, 18, 48
Full BFA membership, 31

health and safety, 94
hire purchase, 58

independent advice, 64, 81, 111
initial fees, 57, 71
insurance, 90
intellectual property, 78
internet, 35
investment franchise, 13

job franchise, 12

lease purchase, 58, 62
limited company, 85, 86
location, 49, 70
long-term objectives, 105

management
    fees, 71
    franchise, 13
market prices, 63
Memorandum of Association,
    86
meeting the franchisor, 72
monitoring your market, 101

National Franchise Forum, 33
NI, 92, 93

obligations, 79
ongoing fees, 57, 71
operating
    lease, 58
    manual, 97–99
operational controls, 79
organisational structure, 67
overdraft, 61

partnership, 85, 86
PAYE, 92, 93
period of contract, 79
pilot franchises, 66
premises, 57, 70
professional advice, 81, 112–
    114
profitability, 109–110

profit and loss account, 87
prospectus, 46
Provisional BFA membership,
    31
public liability insurance, 90
purchase agreement, 75

raising capital, 59
redundancy, 94
renewal
    charge, 82
    fee, 82
renewing franchise agreement,
    82
researching franchising, 34–36
retail franchise, 13
rights of franchisee, 78
royalty fees, 71

sales
    and distribution franchise,
        13
    forecasts, 111
selling your franchise, 18, 79
seminars, 45
shortlisting opportunities, 40
Small Firms Loan Guarantee
    Scheme, 62
sole trader, 84, 86
sources of finance, 60–61
start-up costs, 50, 55, 82

termination of franchise
    agreement, 80
training, 96

unfair dismissal, 92
United Kingdom Franchise
    Directory, 35

VAT, 87

working capital, 58